Letts

GCSE Success

Revision Guide

English &
English Literature

Frank Fitzsimons • John Mannion

Contents

Punctuation and oral work

Writing and the media

Shakespeare

Poetry

Novels and short stories

Exam advice

KK

Course requirements

These pages show how your course is structured, how to begin your revision and advice for catch-up assignments. You also need to be aware whether you are entered for both exams – English and English Literature.

English language coursework

In English, coursework accounts for 40% of your final grade.

- 20% for Speaking and Listening
- 20% for Reading and Writing

In English Literature, coursework accounts for 30% of the grade.

The good news is that for some units you are allowed to submit the same coursework for both exams. These are called 'crossover units'.

For the English exam you will be assessed in the following areas:

Speaking and Listening EN1

There will be THREE orals:

- Individual Extended Contribution
- Drama Focus
- Group

Your teacher will match each of them with following sets of skills:

| Explain Describe Narrate | Explore Analyse Imagine | Discuss Argue Persuade |

English language

Reading EN2

There are two coursework responses to Reading (EN2) and two responses to Writing (EN3):

- Shakespeare (EN2) possible crossover (5%)
- Prose Study (EN2) possible crossover (5%)
- Media (EN3 analyse, review, comment) (5%)
- Original/Personal Writing (EN3) (5%) (Imagine, explore, entertain.)

Notice that the two EN assignments are crossover assignments. This means that they will get you the literature mark as well.

Shakespeare – There is no set play so you will follow the teacher's choice.

Prose study – If it is to be a crossover assignment for Literature, the text must date before 1914 and be by an author recognised by the National Curriculum. There is a wider choice if it is not used as a crossover.

Writing (EN3)

Media – This assignment can range from a comparative analysis of two adverts to the film language of a film trailer.

Original writing – you could be asked to write a story, a number of poems or a piece of non-fiction, such as travel writing.

Exams form 60% of your grade

Reading EN2

Unseen
Media and non-fiction texts   15%
Prepared Texts
Poems from different cultures and traditions 15%

Writing EN3

Writing to advise, inform, explain or describe 15%
Writing to argue, persuade or advise   15%

English literature

Coursework forms 30% of the final grade.
- Pre-1914 Drama – Shakespeare (crossover) 10%
- Pre-1914 Prose (crossover) 10%
- Post-1914 Drama 10%

Exams form 70% of your grade
- Set texts – 30%
- Poems in the English literary heritage – 40%

Revision checklist

☑ Do you understand the exam requirements of your course(s)?

☐ Have you looked over past exam papers? Ask your teacher for past exam papers fairly early in your revision. Try answering a few of them while timing yourself. Brainstorm answers to past questions.

☐ Have you completed all your coursework? You cannot get a good grade unless all your coursework is completed.

☐ Have you produced a revision timetable? **Time management** is crucial at every stage in your revision and not just in the exams themselves. You will relieve the pressure on yourself if you manage your time properly and leave yourself time to relax.

☐ Eat properly and go to bed in good time and don't be tempted to stay up too late doing last minute revision.

☐ Do you stick to your revision timetable? A little and often is better for the mind than doing a lot rarely.

☐ Do you revise actively? Pair up with a friend if this helps motivate you. You can share the work and report your findings to each other. Why not proof read each other's work? You will get better at spotting your mistakes! Devise memory triggers such as mnemonics: the letters of words that help you remember key ideas. Record yourself answering questions, produce mind-maps for key themes, points and ideas.

Catching up on missing assignments

At least one alternative catch-up assignment will be suggested in the coursework sections that follow.

If you use an idea from this book for a catch-up assignment, remember to clear this with your teacher first! Your teacher is the one who has to submit your coursework to the exam board and do all the paperwork!

Course construction

Each Exam Board's Syllabus approaches the coursework and exam requirements of the Department for Education in slightly different ways. Find out which Exam Board you have been entered for and check to understand how your course has been constructed.

Make sure you understand these terms before moving on!

- cross-over
- prose study
- time management

Punctuation again!

- Why? You may be still surviving on skills learned in Year 8.
- You cannot get good grades in English Language unless you can punctuate your writing skilfully and correctly.

Why use punctuation?

Are your skills in punctuation letting you down?
You cannot get high grades in English Language and Literature unless you can punctuate your writing skilfully and correctly. Here's a chance to brush up on these skills.

- When you speak you punctuate naturally through your pauses and body language. However, when you write you have to help your reader understand what you mean through a variety of punctuation marks. The more you know about punctuation the better you will be able to express yourself. Pupils who use semi-colons and colons stand out from others, especially if they use these punctuation marks effectively.

- Writing is a second-hand way of getting your meaning across to others; we need to punctuate our work to help our audience understand us. Remember, when other people read our writing, the words and punctuation we use are the only way we can communicate our message. We are no longer in a position to put right any errors, as we would be if we were speaking directly to our audience.

- To sum up, we use punctuation marks to clarify the points and ideas that we need to communicate to others.

🌐 INTERNET
Here's a great website on punctuation and grammar to extend yourself further.
http://owl.english.purdue.edu/handouts/grammar/

 Markers can miss good points and ideas in your writing when their attention is continually drawn to punctuation errors.

Capital letters

need to be used in the first and main words of titles of books, newspapers, films, groups, programmes, etc.

are used for initials of people's names and places. Remember that 'I' needs one too.

are used for days of the week, months, holidays and special days.

are used as acronyms for organisations: BBC, NATO, and GMTV. Note that you don't need the dot after each letter with well-known organisations.

CAPITAL LETTERS

are used in speech: Julia asked, "Have you begun your revision for English yet?"

have to be used for adjectives from proper (specific) nouns. For instance, English, French, Elizabethan and McDonalds.

begin all sentences and are used at the beginning of lines of verse.

are used when writing letters with "Dear" and "Yours …"

Marks are specifically awarded for punctuation and grammar in your coursework and exam answers – so proof read your work!

KEY TERMS

Make sure you understand these terms before moving on!

- acronyms
- adjectives
- proper nouns

QUICK TEST

1 Why is punctuation necessary?
2 List four areas where you would use capital letters.
3 Correct the following sentences:
   a) "what's the capital of portugal, Anthony?"
   b) my favourite christmas song of all time is "Fairytale of New York" by The Pogues and Kirsty MacColl.
4 Which words need a capital? hamburger restaurant, monday, summer, the atlantic, westlife, rspca, sea, christmas and louise.

End of sentence punctuation

Punctuation helps you express yourself clearly so that you can get your ideas across to others.

Full stops

This is the main punctuation mark that signals the end of one idea and the beginning of another. Sentences help complete ideas in your writing. Use **full stops** to make strong points in your writing as they slow readers down. If you want your readers to mull over what you have to say or if you have an important point to make, use a full stop. If you want your readers to read your ideas quickly, use **semi-colons** or **colons**.

To get high grades in GCSE you will need to vary the length of your sentences and the style of your punctuation.

Change your sentences by making some long and some short; variety is the spice of life and your task is to keep your audience interested in what you want to say. You can add to the variety by using a range of connective words that will also give you a range of expressive possibilities. Try to be expressive through your choice of punctuation. If you want to describe something use semi-colons; if you want to make effective statements and commands use full stops.

Read your work aloud and listen to where one idea ends and another begins. Each idea is a sentence. Trust your ears.

Semi-colons

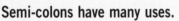

Semi-colons have many uses.

■ They join two or more closely related ideas:

1. Steve worked hard for his results; he stuck to his revision plan.
2. Spring has come early; the trees have begun to blossom and the grassy banks are full of daffodils.
3. There are a number of good movies on tonight; just after the news on ITV they are showing *Clueless*.

■ They separate sets of items in a list when there are commas within the sets or lists:

When you unpack your new computer and set it up you should follow the loose-leaf instructions packed with your computer; you will then, if you look carefully, find everything you need: multi-coloured leads; the plugs for your monitor and base unit; the speakers with their leads; a microphone, if this is included, with a stand; manuals for your computer and, if you are lucky, lots of interesting software.

■ You do not need a capital letter after a semi-colon.

Colons

These are two dots, one above the other, and they signify a new sentence. They are used to:

■ introduce a list:
You should bring to your exam: a watch, two pens, a pencil and a ruler, tissues and hope!

■ introduce quotations:
Hamlet ponders: 'To be or not to be. That is the question.' It is also acceptable to use a comma to introduce this brief quotation from 'Hamlet'.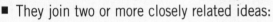

■ punctuate dialogue in plays:
Macbeth: If we should fail?
Lady Macbeth: We fail!
But screw your courage to the sticking place, And we'll not fail.

■ expand on the meaning of a previous idea:
Tracy scored the highest grade in the exam: it was an A star.
A dash can also do the job of a colon by emphasising the sentence that follows:

■ Tom had achieved fantastic results in his exams – he got A stars in five of them.

■ The girls' team won the cup – Phyllis scored the deciding goal.

Other punctuation

Exclamation marks

Exclamation marks help express surprise, anger, fear, joy and most other emotions. For instance: Louise! It is good to see you!

Question marks

These marks can be used for rhetorical questions where no direct reply is expected, only mental agreement: 'Who could defend a statement like that?'. They can also be used for requests for information: 'What time is it?' You do not need a question mark for an indirect question: 'Siobhan asked me for a pen.'

Five things to remember

1. All sentences need punctuation marks to show that they have ended.
2. To get the highest grades in GCSE English you will have to use a wide range of punctuation.
3. Vary the length and style of your sentences to maintain the interest of your audience.
4. Look carefully at how professional writers and authors punctuate their work and try to work out the effects the writers are aiming to produce.
5. If you do not punctuate your work properly, you risk being misunderstood.

Look at how professional writers use punctuation as you read their work. Pause over some passages and think about the effectiveness of the punctuation.

Punctuation practice

Replace the missing punctuation marks from the following extract.

Oh yes I do – I know a lot about 'em I was one myself once though not long – not so long as my clothes they were very long I recollect and always in my way when I wanted to kick why do babies have such yards of unnecessary clothing it is not a riddle I really want to know I never could understand it is it that the parents are ashamed of the size of the child and wish to make believe that it is longer than it actually is I asked a nurse once why it was she said lor sir they always have long clothes bless their little hearts and when I explained that her answer although doing credit to her feelings hardly disposed of my difficulty she replied lor sir you wouldn't have em in short clothes poor little dears and she said it in a tone that seemed to imply I had suggested some family outrage

From *Idle Thoughts of an Idle Fellow, On Babies,* Jerome K Jerome, Essays, 1889

Your punctuation can be checked against the original, here: http://www.literaturepage.com/read/idlethoughts.html

Make sure you understand these terms before moving on!

- full stops
- semi-colons
- colons
- exclamation marks

KEY TERMS

QUICK TEST

1. Which are the quickest to get through when reading: full stops or semi-colons? *Semi-colons*
2. Explain one of the things that semi-colons can do. *was quickest to get*
3. What is a sentence?
4. Can a colon introduce a list of items?
5. Can colons be used to introduce a quotation?
6. Give one other purpose for a colon.

Uses for commas

The skilful use of punctuation marks can improve your expression.

Commas

Commas have a variety of uses.

They can be used to separate items in lists:

> I would like three hamburgers, a cheeseburger,
> a large serving of fries and a coffee.

They are used to clarify sentences that could be misleading:

> After a period of calm, students returned after the fire alarm.

They need to be used in **direct speech**:

> Elaine was curious about the previous evening and asked, 'Where did you get to?'
> 'The shopping centre,' John replied.

They can be used to mark off words, phrases, and connectives in sentences:

> Billy, who did not like to be made fun of, was angry.
> On the other hand, there was no harm in what Carly said.

We use commas, naturally when we speak, but be careful not to use them instead of full stops in sentences.

Whether you use double inverted commas or single ones in your direct speech – be consistent.

Comma practice

Try your skills by putting back the missing commas in this passage from one of the earliest novels.
I was born in the year 1632 in the city of York of a good family though not of that country my father being a foreigner of Bremen who settled first at Hull. He got a good estate by merchandise and leaving off his trade lived afterwards at York from whence he had married my mother whose relations were named Robinson a very good family in that country and from whom I was called Robinson Kreutznaer; but by the usual corruption of words in England we are now called – nay we call ourselves and write our name – Crusoe; and so my companions always called me.

I had two elder brothers one of whom was lieutenant-colonel to an English regiment of foot in Flanders formerly commanded by the famous Colonel Lockhart and was killed at the battle near Dunkirk against the Spaniards. What became of my second brother I never knew any more than my father or mother knew what became of me.

Daniel Defoe, Robinson Crusoe, Chapter 1

Check the website to see how your use of commas compares with Daniel Defoe's here:

http://www.literature.org/authors/defoe-daniel/robinson-crusoe/chapter-01.html

Speech marks

Speech

There are four rules for setting out speech:

1. Use **inverted commas** for the words spoken: Catherine said, 'I haven't seen you in ages!'
2. Direct speech must be separated from the rest of the writing by a punctuation mark. See comma in the example above.
3. Remember to use a capital letter when you begin the direct speech: Catherine said, 'It's ages since I last saw you.'
4. **Each time you introduce a new speaker begin a new line and indent.** That is, begin the speech of your new speaker three letter spaces to the right of the margin.

Quotation marks

- These are inverted commas for words or phrases cited from texts. Stick with single inverted commas for speech and double inverted commas for speech within speech. For instance: Jane shouted to her husband in the next room, 'Your mother phoned and she said, "When are you going to visit me?" Colin, I thought that you called in on her last week.'

- Remember to close them. To show that you are ending a quotation, place the final full stop on the outside of the inverted comma as with the following example. In *My Fair Lady*, Eliza Doolittle shows her independence from Professor Higgins when she says, 'I can do without you'.

Title marks

- In secondary schools inverted commas are used to signify: book titles, stories, newspapers, magazines, television programmes, movies or shows. For example, 'My Fair Lady' is the title of the musical or 1964 film version of the play, 'Pygmalion'.

- In your writing always use title marks to show the difference between **eponymous characters** and the names of the plays and novels in which they appear: Macbeth is a character whereas 'Macbeth' is a play. (Eponymous characters share their name with the titles of their texts.)

- The **convention** (or accepted rule) for titles in universities is to underline them: <u>Hamlet</u> and <u>Macbeth</u>. The main thing is to remain consistent in your method of identifying titles.

- Note that if you use **italics for titles** then this is acceptable for printed work. Notice that in much of this book italics have been used for the titles of texts and films.

KEY TERMS

- commas
- direct speech
- inverted commas
- quotation marks
- title marks
- eponymous characters
- convention
- italics for titles

QUICK TEST

1. Identify three uses for commas.
2. Write a sentence in which you need an exclamation mark.
3. Do you need a question mark for indirect or reported speech?
4. Make up a sentence in which you use all four rules for setting out speech.
5. What do you need to use when you write out the title of a film, book, story, etc. ?

Apostrophes

They help shorten words or show that something belongs to someone.

Apostrophes that show possession

Possessive pronouns

Possessive pronouns do not need apostrophes to show ownership:

- my
- his
- hers
- yours
- its
- ours
- theirs

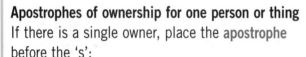

Examples

The computer is hers.
The watch is mine.
The house is theirs.
The bag is yours.

Apostrophes of ownership for one person or thing

If there is a single owner, place the **apostrophe** before the 's':

- Tim's video player
- Christine's house
- The sun's rays

Apostrophes of ownership for more than one owner

If there is more than one owner, you need to put the apostrophe after the 's' to show that you mean a plural owner:

- The Jacksons' video
- The Smiths' house

If a person's name naturally ends in 's' you can do one of two things:

- James's haircut

or

- James' haircut
- The Jones's house

Whichever style you go for, stick with it because readers and markers like you to remain consistent.

If a plural noun does not need an 's' to make it plural, you should place your apostrophe before the 's':

- The men's business venture
- The women's society
- The children's playground
- The people's champion

Expression

You can vary your expression by using an apostrophe:

- 'The claws of the cat' becomes 'The cat's claws' with an apostrophe.

If you are unsure of where to put a possessive apostrophe then write your sentence the long way round:

- 'Dan's new house' becomes 'The new house of Dan'.

Always ask yourself why you are inserting an apostrophe. Do not put it in just for good measure.

 Its and it's can be confusing words. If you wrote, 'I emptied a box of its contents', you would not need an apostrophe. This is because 'its' in this instance is a possessive pronoun. On the other hand if you say, 'It's going to rain all day', you need an apostrophe because you mean 'it is'.

 Abbreviated words are to be used only in informal writing. We use them when we speak or write to friends or family. Avoid using shortened words in your assignments and exams unless you are asked to do so.

Apostrophes that shorten words

- **Contractions** combine two words into one with an apostrophe.
- Abbreviations are words in which letters have been missed out. Apostrophes are used to show that one or more letters have been missed out.

> I'm = I am   Won't = Will not
> Doesn't = Does not   They're = They are
> Can't = Cannot   Would've = Would have

Use an apostrophe when writing the time
- 'I will see Dave at 7 o'clock.' This is the short way of writing 'seven of the clock'.
- Missing numbers in dates can be suggested by an apostrophe:
  21st of September '99
  3rd of November '01

Apostrophes in plays

Playwrights such as Shakespeare shortened their words to allow their verse to remain in iambic pentameter. Shakespeare tried to divide his blank-verse lines into 10 syllables, that is, five feet of two syllables each. Take this example from *Romeo and Juliet*, in which Romeo wants Juliet to exchange vows:
- Romeo: Th' exchange of thy love's faithful vow for mine.

Apostrophes in dialect

Apostrophes are used a great deal by writers when they try to represent local dialect:
' 'ow's it goin' me ole mate?'
' 'awight, 'ow's it goin' yurself? I aint seen yu' in ages!'

🌐 INTERNET

Still confused by apostrophes?
If you would like to know about apostrophes and how they have been used and abused over the centuries try this interesting article by Rosemarie Ostler, The Apostrophe Conundrum

http://www.sharpwriter.com/aaacontent/apostrophe.htm

Apostrophes are marks that help readers understand the intention of the writer. Use them to convey meaning as fully as you can.

KEY TERMS

Make sure you understand these terms before moving on!
- apostrophe
- possessive pronouns
- contractions

QUICK TEST

True or false?
1. Possessive pronouns can take apostrophes.
2. Apostrophes lengthen words.
3. Apostrophes can help show ownership.
4. If a person's name ends with an 's' you can put the apostrophe after it.
5. I ca'nt is correct.
6. Apostrophes of possession can help vary your sentences and can make them shorter.

Sentences

Sentence types

The four types of sentence in English are: simple, compound, complex and minor.

Simple sentences must contain:
- a subject (the person or thing doing the action) e.g. Helen, the cat, I, They, the mad old professor
- a verb (the action) e.g. running, listens, slept, was alarmed.

They can have other parts as well:
- objects (the person or thing acted upon), e.g. The dog ate *the biscuit*
- complements (additional information about the subject) e.g. Fadela is a *doctor*.
- adverbials (additional information about the verb) e.g. *quickly, on Tuesday, at the house*.

When they form part of other sentences, simple sentences are usually referred to as clauses.

Compound sentences join two or more sentences together. The two parts are joined by coordinating conjunctions such as 'and', 'but' or 'or'.
e.g. Ben went to the cinema but I stayed at home.
Do you want to catch the bus or will you walk home?

Complex sentences have two or more clauses joined by subordinating conjunctions such as 'although', 'because' and 'if'. The main clause makes sense on its own. The subordinate clause does not make sense on its own. The subordinate clause follows the subordinating conjunction.
e.g. I didn't see you at the party although I looked everywhere.
If you read in this light, you'll hurt your eyes.

Note that the subordinate clause can occur at the beginning of the sentence as well as at the end.

Minor sentences usually consist of a single verb or verb phrase. They are often used in instructions.
e.g. Shut up!
No smoking.

 Examiners are looking for a variety of sentences in your writing. Avoid too many sentences joined by coordinating conjunctions and remember that short, sharp sentences can be very effective.

Variety within sentences

As well as using all the different sentence types, examiners will be impressed if you vary the internal structure of your sentences. Two ways of doing this involve:
- Placing the most important information at the beginning of the sentence
- Withholding important information until the end to create suspense.

For instance:
Passing my driving test was probably one of the proudest moments of my life.
places emphasis on the passing of the test, whereas the sentence
One of the proudest moments of my life was probably passing my driving test
uses exactly the same words but places the emphasis on how the speaker felt.

Even quite simple sentences can be rearranged according to what you are paying attention to.
The dog bit the man focuses on the dog.
The man was bitten by the dog focuses on the man.
The man was bitten eliminates the dog completely and places more emphasis on the biting.

The last two examples are examples of passive constructions.

The passive voice

The passive voice places emphasis on the thing done rather than the person or thing performing an action. It uses part of the verb 'to be' such as 'is' or 'was' plus a past participle such as 'heard' or 'taken'
e.g. Two pills are to be taken twice per day.
    The glass was broken.

The passive voice can be very useful for avoiding responsibility
The glass was broken is much more likely to get you off the hook than *I broke the glass*.
Or when the person who performed an action is not known
The wheel was discovered thousands of years ago.
Or when the actor is not important as in a scientific experiment
The measurements were taken at regular intervals.

But ... Overuse of the passive should be avoided. Writing is rather flat if you don't know who is doing what. Passive sentences can sound over formal and they can be confusing.
For instance *The enemy's throat was cut with a dagger* is rather less exciting than *I cut my enemy's throat with a dagger.*

 A recent survey showed that A* candidates used the most simple sentences and made good noun and verb choices.
C candidates often 'overloaded' sentences with too many adjectives.
D candidates tended to overuse compound sentences and used too many pronouns.

Pronouns in sentences

Pronouns are words that stand in for nouns, e.g. I, you, he, she, it, we, they, him, her, its, himself. Pronouns are very useful but they can cause a number of problems. In a compound sentence it makes sense not to repeat the noun. Aaron read the book and then he wrote a review.
is better than: Aaron read the book and then Aaron wrote a review.

BUT you can overuse this technique and if there is more than one character involved it can be confusing.
Can you understand the following sentence?
    Patrick gave the CD to Joe but he was annoyed when he didn't tell him that he had recorded it.

KEY TERMS

Make sure you understand these terms before moving on!

- simple sentences
- compound sentences
- complex sentences
- minor sentences
- the passive voice
- pronouns

QUICK TEST

True or false?
1. A phrase can be a sentence.
2. Independent clauses can make sense on their own.
3. 'When you look into them' is a sentence.
4. The sentence, 'Write your name in block capitals' is a statement.
5. Varying your sentences can improve your expression.

Spellings

Methods for learning tricky spellings

- The first piece of advice seems obvious, yet it is surprising how little it is taken – look up words in dictionaries and check their spellings. Dictionaries work on the alphabet principle for each word and finding words becomes easier with practice. Carry a small dictionary with you. Relying on teachers and others to spell words for you means that you will never really learn them. Aim to be an independent learner.

- The Look–Say–Cover–Write–Check method is a successful one as long as you have spelled the word correctly in the first place. Learning words by repeating this process does work.

- Try writing a crazy but memorable sentence using each letter of the word (a mnemonic). Take for example, the word believe. Big elephants look inside elephantine vases everywhere. Only use this method for the few words that are the biggest bugbears for you, otherwise you will have too many strange phrases to remember.

- Use the sound of words to help you spell them. Work your way through each syllable as you aim to spell the word. This works for many words and is always worth trying before using other methods.

- For tricky plural endings follow the rules in 5, 6 and 7. If a noun ends with a 'y' and it has a letter such as 't', 'r' or 'n' before the y, you need to add 'ies' to the plural.
  Example diary – diaries, curry – curries, company – companies, city – cities

- If the last letter before the 'y' is a vowel (a, e, i, o, u) you have to add an 's' to make the plural.
  Example boy – boys, journey – journeys, key – keys, guy – guys, monkey – monkeys

- Words which end in 'fe' such as knife take 'ves' in plurals; similarly, words ending in 'f' like shelf or half change to shelves and halves in plurals.

- Use 'i' before 'e' except after 'c'.
  For example, receive.

  Proof read your work for words that you know you are likely to get wrong. Make a list of these words from a number of subjects and focus on learning them.

Word families

A good way of improving your spelling is to realise that words belong to families. If you know the basic word you will have a good idea about other similar words. For instance, the spelling of criticism is easier if you relate it to critic. Here are some other useful word families.

act, actor, action, activity react, reaction

assist, assistant, assistance

balance, imbalance, unbalanced

bore, boring, boredom

call, recall, calling

claim, reclaim, reclamation, disclaim

child, children, childhood, childlike, childish, childless

cover, discover, discovery, uncover

critic, criticism, criticise, critique

electric, electrical, electricity, electrician, electronic, electrocute

examine, examination, examiner, examinee

fill, fulfil, fulfilling, fulfilment, give, given, forgive, forgiveness

govern, governor, government

hand, handler, handy, handicraft

hero, heroic, heroism

joy, joyful, enjoy, enjoyment

light, lightening, delighted, enlighten

machine, machinery, machinist

medic, medical, medication

native, nation, national, nativity

nature, natural, unnatural, denatured

obey, disobey, disobedient

operate, operator, cooperate, cooperation

pack, packet, package

pain, painkiller, painful, painless, painstaking
pass, passage, passenger

press, impress, depression, repress, express

prison, imprison, imprisonment

prove, approval, disapprove,

public, publication, publicity, publicise

relate, relative, relation

shake, shakily, shaken

sign, signatory, signature, signal, resign, resignation

sum, summary, summation, assume, assumption

syllable, monosyllable, monosyllabic, polysyllabic

take, mistake, mistaken, overtaken, overtaking, partaking

QUICK TEST

1. What is the difference between an examiner and an examinee?
2. Can you think of any other words that make this distinction?
3. Can you explain why fulfil and fulfilment are spelt differently from fulfilling?

Words often misspelt

Words often misspelt

A–F

accommodation
alcohol
although
analyse
analysis
argument
assessment
atmosphere
audience
beautiful
beginning
believe
beneath
business
caught
chocolate
column
conclusion
conscience
consequence
continuous
creation
daughter
decide
decision
definite
design
development
diary
disappear
disappoint

embarrass
engagement
enquire
environment
evaluation
evidence
February
fierce
forty
fulfil
furthermore

G–P

guard
happened
health
height
imaginary
improvise
interesting
interrupt
issue
jealous
knowledge
listening
lonely
lovely
marriage
material
meanwhile
miscellaneous

mischief
moreover
murmur
necessary
nervous
original
outrageous

P–R

parallel
participation
peaceful
people
performance
permanent
persuade
persuasion
physical
possession
preparation
prioritise
process
proportion
questionnaire
queue
reaction
receive
reference
relief
remember
research

S–W

safety
Saturday
secondary
separate
sequence
shoulder
sincerely
skilful
soldier
stomach
straight
strategy
strength
success
surely
surprise
survey
technique
technology
texture
tomorrow
unfortunately
Wednesday
weight
weird
women

Remind yourself of the spelling techniques that are set out on page 16.

Synonyms

These are words that mean the same.

Examples
beautiful = pretty, nice, fine, good-looking, elegant, lovely, fair
display = show, exhibit, exhibition, spread, open, expose, demonstration, layout

Common homophones and confusions

a lot, allot
never alot as a single word

advise, advice
to advise, to give advice

affect, effect
to influence, a result

allowed, aloud
permitted, out loud

are, our
part of the verb to be, belonging to us

bean, been
as in baked bean, part of the verb to be

beech, beach
tree, seashore

blue, blew
colour, air moved

board, bored
wood or group of managers, uninterested

bought, brought
purchased, carried

break, brake
damage, slow down

by, buy, bye
next to or responsible for, purchase, farewell

cell, sell
enclosed space, dispose of for money

cent, scent, sent
coin, smell, dispatched

cereal, serial
type of grain, a story in parts

choose, chose
decide – present tense, decide – past tense

cloth, clothe
material, to dress

conscience, conscious
sense of right or wrong, aware

course, coarse
route or direction, rough

dear, deer
beloved or expensive, mammal

fate, fête
inevitable force, celebration

flour, flower
bread ingredient, part of plant

grate, great
scrape, very large

hair, hare
on head, animal

herd, heard
group, listened to

here, hear
this place, listen

him, hymn
that man, religious song

hole, whole
pit, complete

hour, our
time, belonging to us

it's, its
it is, belonging to it

key, quay
lock opener, boat dock

knight, night
wears armour, darkness

knot, not
rope tie or nautical speed, negative

know, no
be aware, negative

made, maid
built or done, female worker

main, mane
important or the sea, lion's hair

meet, meat
come together, animal flesh

might, mite
possibly or strength, small insect or small amount

morning, mourning
early part of day, marking a death

new, knew
recent, was aware

pane, pain
part of window, hurt

peace, piece
quiet, segment or part

place, plaice
location, fish

plane, plain
flat (in maths) or short for airplane, not beautiful or large expanse of flat land

practise, practice
to practise, a practice

quiet, quite
not loud, fairly

read, reed
activity with text, sort of grass

rein, rain, reign
horse equipment, water, royal rule

right, write
correct, use pen

rode, road, rowed
used vehicle, carriageway, used oars

scene, seen
part of play, looked at

see, sea
look, body of water

sew, so, sow
use needle and thread, intensifier, scatter seed

sites, sights
places, things seen or aiming device

source, sauce
origin, food supplement

stair, stare
steps, look hard

steel, steal
metal, take

sum, some
total, a few

sun, son
thing in sky, male descendant

tail, tale
part of animal, story

their, they're, there
belonging to them, they are, that place

too, two, to
in addition, 2, in the direction of

vain, vein
self admiring, blood vessel

waist, waste
below stomach, not used

week, weak
seven days, without strength

where, were, wear
which place, used to be, clothe

you, yew, ewe
person, tree, female sheep

you're, your
you are, belonging to you

Punctuation and oral work

Linking words and phrases

Putting your ideas in the right order

Words that help put your ideas in order
- firstly, then, so far, secondly, in the end, next, eventually, subsequently, at last, at length, afterwards

Words for exceptions
- only, if, unless, except (for), save for

Making points and giving examples

Words to use to argue and make points
- consequently, thus, so, as a result, because, as, hence, therefore, since, until, whenever, accordingly, as long as

Words to help you give examples
- for example, for instance, such as, take the case of, thus, as (evidence), to show that, as revealed by

Words for extra points or ideas
- and, too, what is more, also, furthermore, and then, again, moreover, as well as, in addition

Words which help you emphasise points
- above all, in particular, notably, specifically, indeed, more important, especially, significant(ly), in fact

Paragraphing

Paragraphs are necessary to give the readers a rest and help them to follow the writer's meaning.
- **Paragraphs** are groups of sentences connected by the same topic. Each paragraph carries a main idea.

- The main sentence of a paragraph is often found at the beginning and it is called a **topic sentence**. For example: *Successful students plan their revision in each subject. They plan how much time they have available and then try to cover a number of areas in each subject.*

- Any paragraphs following the first paragraph will need to begin on a new line, indented 2 cm from the page margin. In business correspondence or word-processed work there is no need to indent new paragraphs.

- You can link your paragraphs together skilfully by using the **connecting words** found in the boxes on these pages.

Being persuasive and analytical

Words to persuade
- of course, naturally, obviously, clearly, certainly, surely, evidently

Words to help you show an opinion or analyse
- it would seem, to suggest, one might conclude/propose/deduce/infer/imply/say/consider

Comparing and contrasting

Words to make a contrast or show what is different
- but, nevertheless, alternatively, despite this, on the contrary, however, yet, the opposite, instead, whereas, to turn to, although, still, on the other hand

Words to compare things in your writing OR SHOW what is the same
- equally, in the same way, as with, likewise, similarly, compared with, an equivalent

Essay endings

Words to sum up or end with
- in brief, in summary, throughout, in all, on the whole, to sum up, overall, finally, to conclude, to recap, in the end

Practice

Insert appropriate linking words and phrases in this passage so that it flows and makes sense

My friends object when I buy supermarket eggs laid by caged hens. _____ they tell me that I have "no social conscience!" _____ they say that it is people like me who perpetuate the hens' suffering by buying these eggs. _____ I tell them that I have always done so out of habit. _____ I do not want the birds to suffer.

_____ I had not considered the egg industry and how some hens were allowed to roam free. _____ reading up on the subject I have decided to change my buying habits. _____ with the cost of groceries going up I would appreciate a pay rise before I do so. _____ not everyone can afford to buy free range.

KEY TERMS

Make sure you understand these terms before moving on!

- paragraphs
- topic sentences
- connecting words

QUICK TEST

1. Why use paragraphs?
2. Identify two words that can help you compare pieces of writing.
3. What is the difference between comparing and contrasting?
4. Give two words that help emphasise points in writing.
5. What do these words help you to do: 'furthermore' and 'moreover'?

Improving writing style

The ideas on these pages should enable you to write more effectively and improve your EN3 grade. (Writing)

Ways to improve your writing style

Vocabulary and choice of words

Firstly, think about the words you choose. Your words need to be appropriate for the text and as accurate as possible. When one of your characters gets into a car, does she get into a battered old Ford, a people carrier or an oversized all-terrain vehicle? Do your characters say things all the time or do they mutter, mumble or shout?

Varying sentence length and paragraphs

You already know about different types of sentences, but you should also think about the rhythm of your writing. Large stretches of long sentences can give a sense of continuity and flow, but they can become monotonous. Try short sentences for emphasis. Even more emphatic than the short sentence is the short paragraph.

A single sentence paragraph can really stand out.

Building tension

You can, for example, build a tense atmosphere by keeping your sentences short. For example, in a horror story you could show fear and **tension** through using short, darting sentences.

'I ran. Ran for all I was worth! Sometimes I stumbled over tree roots. Branches slashed my face. Twigs and branches snapped under the weight of the creature rushing behind me. A savage, wolf-like howl shredded the air. Moments later it seized and bit my left foot! 'God help me!' I screamed, as I turned to see what was attacking me'.

Varying sentence structures

The first part of a sentence tends to contain the subject. In the middle of a piece of writing this is often known information – the new information comes at the end. From time to time you can vary this order. Compare the impact of:

As I put the car in gear the engine went 'thunk'.

With

'Thunk' went the engine as I put the car into gear.

You can also make choices when it comes to the placing of **adverbial phrases**. These tell you about things like time, mood and manner. For instance:

With deliberate slowness, Dr Shrike marked out the area he was going to cut.

Dr Shrike, with deliberate slowness, marked out the area he was going to cut.

Dr Shrike marked out the area he was going to cut with deliberate slowness.

 Examiners are looking for 'control' in your writing. If you apply most of the ideas on these pages you will have greater control over your writing.

Some pitfalls to avoid

Do not confuse big words with a sophisticated style. Remember that you want to give your readers as clear a picture as possible.

Do not overdo any effect. If all your sentences have an unusual structure, people will find it distracting.

Use figurative language sparingly. One well-chosen simile or metaphor will stand out like a rose in a desert.

Circumlocutions

Circumlocutions are round about ways of saying things. Again stick to the simple word or expression, as this is more effective.

few in number = few
in less than no time = quickly
in the event that = if
on the grounds that = because

Clarity and brevity

Keep what you write brief, simple and clear. Avoid longwinded, pompous sentences.

'I remained in my abode and passed the time watching uninteresting programmes while looking at the little box in the corner.'
Is tedious. Try this instead:
'I stayed at home watching boring programmes on TV.'

Clichés

Clichés are tired expressions and imagery that have lost their impact through gross overuse.

'Like two ships that pass in the night.'
'food for thought', 'leaves much to be desired', 'shoot oneself in the foot'.

Unnecessary repetition

Avoid using tautologies; that is repeating your self unnecessarily. Try also to avoid reinforcing words with words that would be better left out. Your writing will have more impact without them.

Examples of tautologies to avoid are:
final end
sad misfortune
puzzling mystery

Examples of word-reinforcement to avoid:
totally wrong
absolutely fantastic

Overworked words

Avoid overworked words. This is because they can be boring and repetitive.

Examples:

got, get, nice, good, totally, nice, a lot of, kind of, etc. (These words are too casual to be used in formal, standard English.)

Make sure you understand these terms before moving on!

- tension
- adverbial phrases
- control in your writing
- circumlocutions
- clichés
- tautologies

QUICK TEST

1. Reduce these phrases to one word:
(a) Due to the fact that
(b) Pink in colour
(c) In this day and age

2. What is the danger of overdoing description?

3. Identify a cliché and explain why you should try to avoid clichés in writing.

Speaking and listening

To achieve the highest grades you will need to show that you can do the following:

Listening

Listen with sensitivity and respond accordingly.

Carry forward the arguments of others by following and responding to complex speech.

Show ability in handling a wide range of roles in discussion.

Involve and engage listeners by using rhetorical questions, speaking with irony, making thought-provoking contributions and displaying a wide vocabulary. In other words, show flair.

Speech

Speak with sensitivity, fluency and confidence. Think before you speak in groups and use no more than eight words as prompts for your 'extended contribution'. Do not make the mistake of reading notes as this will earn you no marks for speaking and listening.

Initiate speech, sustain a point of view, help shape and manage discussion, synthesise essential points, encourage the participation of others, respond to points with authority and make dynamic and influential contributions.

Technique

Speak with purpose in a structured way. Try to signpost your talk by giving it a clear introduction with obvious, vocal subheadings so your audience can follow your talk.

Use standard English vocabulary and grammar in an assured or mature manner. Study the box below if you do not fully understand what **standard English** is and when to use it.

Vary the sound of your voice to interest your audience. Remember to use eye contact and other forms of **body language** to interest your listener. Most human communication is non-verbal! This means that body language such as body-posture, hand gestures, eye contact and the tone and pitch

of your voice also convey messages when you speak.

In drama-focused activities can you create a complex role and make inventive use of a range of appropriate techniques to direct the response of the audience?

Adapt the **register** of your speech to the task and your audience. You would hardly speak to your head-teacher using the same tone of voice as you would to your best friends!

If appropriate, sprinkle your speech with humour as this wins audiences over but take care not to overdo it.

Standard English

This is formal English. The English you should use with people that you do not know. The aim is to be clearly understood by anyone. Teachers usually use it and so do newscasters. Therefore, do not use 'I should of' or 'I ain't ' when 'I should have' and 'I have not' are called for.

In formal situations avoid your local **dialect**. This should be used only for talking to your family, friends or neighbours. There is nothing wrong with your local dialect. It is the correct, friendly language to use in informal situations. Use it when you talk to your friends and family. It's right then to say, 'Me and my mates are going uptown'.

The three orals

Possible coursework activities	explain describe narrate	explore analyse imagine	discuss argue persuade
Individual extended contribution	A hobby or interest. The rules of a game. A journey or an event. An account of a film or play.	Your life in five years time. Interpret the motives and attitudes of a narrator/ character from a novel, play or poem that you know.	Debate an issue in the news. Give a talk on a controversial subject.
Drama focus	Create a dramatic monologue for an important character from a play, novel or poem. Try to include relevant themes and ideas. Then explain your choices and decisions.	Simulate an interrogation based on a crime from a poem, novel, etc. Change a scene from a play or an incident from a novel and role-play a character in the new situation. Explore what happens.	Speak for a minute for three items on 'Room 101'. Audience to ask questions after each item.
Group	A presentation on an issue at an assembly. Give a presentation of the main themes, ideas, characters of a story, play or film.	Characters from different texts meeting each other in a new context. Explore an issue such as homelessness or education from various points of view.	Debate an issue in the news. Debate the issue of identity cards.

KEY TERMS

Make sure you understand these terms before moving on!

- standard English
- body language
- register
- dialect

QUICK TEST

1. Identify the three types of orals in which you must speak.
2. What is standard English and when should you use it?
3. Why would you use body language?
4. With whom would you use dialect?
5. Why is it important to listen?

Preparing and giving a talk

Planning

First steps

- Think of a suitable title for the talk that you have agreed with your teacher. This will help you focus on your topic. If you need ideas for what you can talk about look again at suggested tasks on page 25.
- Research your topic. Talk to experts; do some research on the Internet; look in encyclopaedias; check out your library; write to companies, agencies, companies or embassies, etc.
- Gather resources to help you with your details, points and arguments. Find and prepare any props that you need now. They will be useful for keeping your audience's attention and focusing them on what you are saying.

The structure

- Summarise the talk in a few paragraphs. Does it have a beginning, middle and an end?
- You could even spider-gram your talk on a page of A-4 to get a visual idea of its structure.

The prompts

- Write down your main ideas in words or phrases on small cards to help remind you of what you intend to say. Eight words or mini phrase should be enough. Remember, these cards are only to serve as **prompts**, you must not read to your audience!
- Write the words or phrases twice the size of your normal writing. This is for your own self-assurance as you speak. A sparse mind-map with coloured sections with big writing and images also works well.
- For **structure**, spread your cards on a table and pick them up in the order that you'd like to give your talk. Number the cards for the right order. The structure of your talk will then be clear for you as well as your audience.

Practice

- Practise your talk by trying out its structure and any specialised or unusual vocabulary, so it is clear in your mind.
- Think about the necessity of using standard English and think about any places in your talk where you might pause and welcome questions. Questions could act as ice-breakers and help you relax. You will also be able to appreciate how your audience are responding to your talk.
- Remember to get your props or handouts ready, if you need them, and pack them in your bag the night before you go to school.

Remember to listen carefully. Don't talk over other people. Take turns in speech. However you do need to say something substantial from time to time in group talks, otherwise it will be impossible for your teacher to fully assess you.

Giving the talk

- Try to appear relaxed and confident. Check the list of what teachers are looking and listening for on the previous page.
- Stand up and try to appear lively by modulating your voice. Use the correct register.
- Remember to match your talk to your audience.
- If it is appropriate, use standard English as fluently and confidently as you can.
- Show that you can listen carefully and respond in a detailed manner to questions asked.
- Be prepared to field questions and show your understanding of your topic by answering them. Prepare by thinking about the kind of questions that you could be asked.

Self-**evaluate** your performance afterwards so that you can learn lessons for your next speaking activity. Ask your teacher for the following information, too. What did you do well? What could you have done better? Try to identify two or three areas for improvement so you can improve on your grade next time.

Oral skills: self-evaluation (brief notes)

What I do well
What I need to improve (1)
What I need to improve (2)

Do not read out your notes aloud. You are not being tested on your ability to read. A major aim is to talk in the most fluent and confident manner that you can.

Giving a talk can be stressful

Here are a few thoughts of the famous to help put things into perspective.

"Studies show that fear of public speaking ranks higher than the fear of dying. I guess this means that most people at a funeral would rather be in the coffin than delivering the eulogy." Jerry Seinfeld (US comedian)

"It's quite simple, (public speaking) Say what you have to say and when you come to a sentence with a grammatical ending, sit down." Winston Churchill (Former Prime Minister)

"Be sincere; be brief; be seated." Franklin Delano Roosevelt (A former President of the USA)

KEY TERMS

Make sure you understand these terms before moving on!

- prompts
- structure
- evaluate

QUICK TEST

1. Why is it important to plan your talk?
2. Towards the end of your talk what might you do to involve your audience?
3. What is main thing that you must avoid?

Practice questions

Use the questions to test your progress. Check your answers on page 93.

Punctuation and sentences

1. Try to sum up in a sentence why you need to punctuate your writing.

   ....

2. Identify five instances where you would need a capital letter.

   ....

3. Correct the following sentences by putting in capital letters where they are necessary:
   jemma read *Great Expectations* for her english course-work. she had never read charles dickens before; she may read another one of his novels before easter.

   ....

4. Identify four of the five punctuation marks that can complete a sentence.

   ....

5. Explain one of the uses that semi-colons can serve.

   ....

6. What is a rhetorical question?

   ....

7. Identify one use for colons.

   ....

8. Give three of the four rules of direct speech.

   ....

9. What are the two main purposes of apostrophes?

   ....

10. Where does the apostrophe need to go with plural nouns that do not need an 's' to make them plurals?

   ....

11. Identify three of the four types of sentences.

   ....

12. Point out the main and dependent clauses of this sentence:
    I will go to see the new movie at the cinema as soon I have done the washing up.

   ....

Spelling and expression

13. Point out two methods of learning tricky spellings.

   ....

14. What is before 'e' except after 'c'?

   ....

15. Why do the following plurals end in 'ies'?   twenties, lorries, cities, injuries and berries.

   ....

16. Why do the following plurals end in 's'?   journeys, trolleys, donkeys, chimneys, toys.

   ....

17. What do 'here', 'there' and 'where' have in common?

   ....

18. Correct the following spellings:
    begginning, apperance, intrested, grammer, tonge, definately, neccesity, rythm, sentance.

   ....

19. What are synonyms?

   ....

20. Why are homophones confusing?

....

21. What are connectives?

....

22. What is the purpose of connectives in writing?

....

23. Why is it necessary to use paragraphs?

....

24. What is a topic sentence?

....

25. Briefly explain what 'control' means in writing.

....

26. Reduce this circumlocution to one word: 'on the grounds that'.

....

Speaking and listening

27. How many orals do you need to do?

....

28. What must each of them be?

....

29. What is dialect?

....

30. Identify three dialects that can be found in Britain.

....

31. Briefly explain what is meant by standard English.

....

32. When, where and to whom would you use standard English and your local dialect?

....

33. Identify two things that you should keep a note of once you have given your oral in class.

....

34. Briefly explain what is meant by 'body language'.

....

35. What is 'register' in speech?

....

36. Explain what is meant by 'irony'.

....

37. Why is it important to listen?

....

38. What does the word 'analyse' mean?

....

39. What kinds of assignments are suitable for discussing, arguing and persuading?

....

40. Why is it important that you do not write out long passages for your talk?

....

41. What is meant by 'structure' in a talk?

....

42. Why is it important to self-assess after your talk?

....

How well did you do? ✗ 0–10 Try again   11–20 Getting there   21–32 Good work   33–42 Excellent! ✓

Original writing

What you are expected to do

Your task is to produce a piece of writing that either explores, imagines or entertains for one or more specific audiences. (Your piece could include all the criteria.)

- In this section you will be assessed on the quality of your writing and not on the texts that you have read. There is a wide range of possibilities of what you may write about because there are no restrictions on **form**, **content** or genre.

- The exam boards do not usually specify any particular length for your work in terms of words or pages; however most of them think that around 1000 words should be long enough for an accurate assessment of your work to be made. For example, if you submitted a group of poems and wrote a brief account of their composition that would be fine; but long, wordy, unfocused projects are not wanted. What is most important is that the written piece has clear aims, a specific purpose, a particular audience and that it is effectively written. If your work is convincing and concise then the examiner must give it a high mark.

- Teachers are conscious of the limited time available to cover both coursework and exam elements of the GSCE. Sometimes they try to cover two or more parts of your coursework using the same topic. For instance, it is not unusual for a media assignment on the comparison of two soaps to extend to a group-oral presentation on a new soap opera. Each member of the group might then go on to produce a piece of original writing by composing a short episode of their soap opera. Media assignments can lend themselves to such creative results.

- If you do not like writing stories, you could write an extra chapter for a novel or a scene from a play that you have read. You could, perhaps, write a few diary entries from any major character that impressed you from the texts in your coursework. However, check first that diaries fill the grading criteria for pieces of coursework for your GCSE in Literature.

🌐 INTERNET
Web sites for examples of excellent stories:
http://www.classicreader.com/toc.php/sid.6/
http://www.short-stories.co.uk/

Writer's block?

Here are a few secrets from the professionals

"It's never perfect when I write it down the first time, or the second time, or the fifth time. But it always gets better as I go over it and over it" Jane Yolen

"I'm not a very good writer, but I'm an excellent rewriter." James Michener

"Writing is long periods of thinking and short periods of writing." Ernest Hemingway

"There are three rules to writing fiction. Unfortunately, no one knows what they are." Somerset Maugham

What you can write about

Here are a few suggested tasks that you could choose from for a fictional piece of writing of 1000 words or so for a story; obviously you would use fewer words for poetry.

Produce a few poems or a long poem such as a ballad to retell an interesting story from the news. Read a few ballads such as *The Lady of Shallot* or *The Ballad of Frankie and Johnny* to get an idea of the form and the effect you can gain from repeating lines and using rhyme in quatrains (four-line stanzas). Notice the **rhythm** and **tone** of ballads – in other words, how they sound when read aloud. Could you choose words which would give your poem an appropriate rhythm and tone?

Devise a soap opera and explain the rationale behind its setting, characters, plots and envisaged audience.

Write an extra chapter for a novel.

Write a short horror story with a 'twist in the tale'.

Write an episode or a few detailed scenes for a soap opera.

Write detailed descriptions of people and places with the aim of entertaining and amusing your audience.

Write a one-act play.

Keep an imaginary diary.

How you will be graded

To achieve a good grade from C to A* you will need to:

- write in the appropriate manner for the genre and purpose of your story
- use a varied range of sentences and vocabulary to keep your audience's interest
- keep punctuation accurate and produce logical paragraphs to make your meaning clear
- develop characters and settings within your narrative
- use literary devices such as similes and metaphors effectively
- show assured control in your writing with a wide range of expression to achieve effects
- show an awareness of tone in words and sentences
- be almost faultless in punctuation and spelling
- write with flair and originality
- show that you can be elaborate or concise.

> *Remember that this work is also a dry run for the exam essay. Each piece of writing will need a plan, no matter how brief.*

🌐 INTERNET

If you would like to read an excellent story you will find one here

http://www.bnl.com/shorts

Many of these stories have short time frames. You could do the same thing in your story by writing about a single incident or an episode that lasts for only a few hours.

Here are a few titles to get you going if you are stuck for ideas:

'My Last Day on Earth'
'Strange Meeting'
'Danger in Venice'
'The Visitors'

Make sure you understand these terms before moving on!

- form
- content
- rhythm
- tone

Story planning & writing

How to write and plan a story

Planning

- Brainstorm or do a spidergram of your ideas on a blank sheet of paper. Sometimes stories can come from a character; sometimes they can come from a specific situation such as a shipwreck or a sudden discovery. Once you have a few ideas, try to think of a title because this may help you focus on the **plot** and characterisation of your story.

- The plot is the plan or outline of your story.

- What will be the climax of your plot when your story reaches a crisis? What will be the result of the climax? From whose point of view is the story going to be told?

- Decide if the style of narration is to be in the first or third person. A first-person narrator tells the story from within the story; a third-person narrator stands outside the story. How much will your narrator know and see? Will the third-person narrator be able to know everything that the characters are thinking? These are matters of perspective. Will the narrator be biased or objective in their viewpoint?

Setting

- Where is the story going to be set? Will it be set at home or abroad? Is the story going to be set in the present, future or past?

- Will your story be drawn from everyday life? Perhaps you would prefer a fairy-tale setting drawn from your imagination? How are you going to describe the **setting**? Will you suggest the setting as you write with minor details or will you be more elaborate in the details that you give to describe the setting? If necessary do a little research to make your setting convincing.

Characters

- You will need a main character and two or three other important **characters**. You could include some minor ones, too. Create a brief profile for each character, as this will enable you to be realistic in your portrayal of them. Have a checklist for each one, for example, their age, appearance, habits, job, traits, ambitions, hobbies, likes and dislikes, motivation, etc.

Genre

- Choose a **genre** for your story. Is your story going to be an adventure, detective, love, science-fiction or comedy story? Can you be even more specific within your genre by going for a sub-division within it (for instance, comedy-romance)?

Structure

- Ensure that you have a clear **structure** with a beginning, middle and end to your story.
- You need to bait your story with a good '**hook**' at the beginning to make your readers read on. Perhaps you could begin in the middle of an exciting incident; you could use some unusual description or maybe start from an unusual perspective to intrigue the reader. Look at examples in stories you read.

Will there be a twist in the tale?

- If your story involves suspense try to include 'a twist in the tale', or perhaps give a moral to your story.

Use of Time

- How are you going to tell your story? The **use of time** is important, will you tell your story in a **linear** (straightforward) way or through flashbacks? The plots of most stories, novels and plays are written in a linear manner. Their plots and characters move forward naturally in time. In contrast, a novel such as *Wuthering Heights* (1847) by Emily Brontë moves forwards and backwards in time as various first-person narrators relate significant events in the novel.

> *Remember that the last part of your sentence usually carries most impact so recast your sentences to maximise your impact, in order to give a powerful account of something imagined.*

KEY TERMS

Make sure you understand these terms before moving on!

- plot
- setting
- characters
- genre
- structure
- hook
- use of time
- linear

QUICK TEST

1. How is a first-person narrative told?
2. What does the term 'genre' mean?
3. What do you need at the beginning of a story to keep your readers interested in reading further?
4. What does it mean to be elaborate?
5. How can you make your characters believable?

Non-fiction writing

This means writing to: describe, explain, inform, advise, entertain, report, review, persuade, witness, compare, contrast, request, complain and express feelings. You will be expected to produce pieces of writing like this for coursework and the exam. Remember to consider the form, purpose and audience of your writing.

What you can write about

An autobiographical piece about, say, a memorable trip or holiday that you made with your family; look at magazines which have 'A Day in the Life of Someone'. In some descriptive detail write about a day in your life for a young person's magazine. Think about your audience as you write your piece. Only you can write about your life so write it as well as you can!

This could be:

- a topic that interests you; explain the issue and give your view of it.

- an interesting picture from a newspaper or a magazine; write about it in as much detail as you can.

- a piece of writing in which you give your view on any subject, for example animal experimentation.

- a **discursive** (digressive) essay about two sides of a topical issue in the news.

Always consider the purpose, message, audience and the best form for your writing.

How you will be graded

To achieve grades C to A* you will need to:

- research your chosen topic carefully

- show that your writing is organised and appropriate for your topic

- interest your readers and sustain points

- use an appropriate range of punctuation to make your meaning clear

- be as interesting and original as you can

- use your own words

- give a powerful account of a real experience

- show both elaboration and conciseness in your writing

- use appropriate registers; that is, match your tone and language to your **audience**

- use wide-ranging vocabulary in which syntax, spelling and punctuation is almost faultless

- consciously shape and craft language to achieve sophisticated effects

- use standard written forms in a convincing manner

- produce a well-organised and compelling piece of work.

When grading your work, examiners will take into account that you had more time to prepare and present your coursework and will understand that you have limited time in exams.

Planning

Non-fiction writing plan

- Decide on a topic and think about your target audience. The form of writing that you choose will be determined by the type of audience that you want to reach.
- Think of an appropriate form: an article, essay, letter, etc.
- Do the research: see experts who know the topic; go to libraries; use the Internet; look in encyclopedias; write to associated organisations.
- Make notes on one side of pieces of paper and number the pages. Make a spidergram if you prefer. Instructions on how to produce a spidergram and an example are on pages 56–57.
- Look over your notes and plan your piece of writing on a single sheet. Number your points. Again this could be organised as a brainstorm.
- Remember to write your title when you write or type your first draft. If you hand-write your work, leave every second line blank for proof reading and alterations; it is easier to check your work that way. Always proof read your work for spelling, punctuation and expression. Read the relevant pages in this book for advice.
- Produce your best draft and remember to proof read your work again for the errors that you are likely to make.

 Always produce at least two drafts of your work. Your second draft should be your best one.

Still stuck for ideas

You could write a blog or a weblog on almost any issue or topic that interests you. Here's a useful definition of a "blog" from Wikipedia, the free online encyclopedia:

"A **blog** (or **weblog**) is a website in which messages are posted and displayed with the newest at the top. Like other media, blogs often focus on a particular subject, such as food, politics, or local news. Some blogs function as online diaries. A typical blog combines text, images, and links to other blogs, web pages, and other media related to its topic. Since its appearance in 1995, blogging has emerged as a popular means of communication, affecting public opinion and mass media around the world."

Do check with your teacher to see if it is okay to produce a piece of writing like this; if you go on to write it have a look at successful weblogs first and try to produce a blog of extended length of around 1000 words or so using standard English as appropriate.

KEY TERMS

Make sure you understand these terms before moving on!

- discursive
- audience
- proof reading

QUICK TEST

1. Identify a form of writing suitable for persuasive writing.
2. What does 'discursive' mean?
3. What is it that you are doing when you look over your work again?
4. How many drafts should you make of your work?
5. Identify three places where you could find information for your chosen topic.

How to write essays

Planning

- Examine key words and phrases in the question to help you focus on your answer.

- Read through your notes and any important passages in your text for evidence.

- Brainstorm an essay plan with your essay question in the middle of a blank piece of paper.

- Aim for three or four main arguments and group your points around them. Remember to include page numbers for any **quotations** used because you will need evidence from your text(s) to prove your arguments.

Writing an introduction

One of the best ways of introducing an essay is to sum up briefly what happens in a scene or chapter and then explain your line of argument while referring to the essay's key words and ideas.

An example

Here is an essay title for the popular drama text, *Educating Rita* (1980) by Willy Russell followed by an introductory paragraph that addresses its key words and ideas.

How does Will Russell present the characters Frank and Rita in the opening scene of *Educating Rita*?

In the opening scene of *Educating Rita* a tired academic, Frank, meets his new, lively, 'Open University' student, Rita. The two characters are culturally from different worlds as each continually mistakes the cultural references of the other. Frank is presented as a cautious, middle class, lecturer who drinks too much and is no longer interested in teaching; Rita is presented as a lively young woman lacking in academic confidence but eager to obtain it; she shows her mental agility by 'testing' Frank, saying exactly what she thinks. Frank likes Rita for her life-affirming nature and he decides against changing this through teaching her. However, Rita shows her determination to learn and will accept no other tutor than Frank.

If you were going to write this essay you would need to begin from the second sentence by working through each of the above points on the 'presentation' of these characters with evidence to back up your points and comments on your evidence.

Try also to integrate comments on the **historical context** where appropriate in comments on your evidence. The historical context includes the attitudes, ideas, culture, entertainment and events of a particular period during which a text was written or set.

The main body of your essay

- Work through each main argument from your introduction as fully as you can.
- Once you think that you have proved an argument sufficiently, move on to your next argument. Do not hammer away at the same point for too long.
- Remember that your technique must be: point, evidence and comment.
- Use a wide range of connective words to link your points and arguments together. These words will join up your points and arguments and link your essay together; the skilful use of connectives can help the fluency of arguments in essays and make them easier to read.

💡 *Get an idea of what good essays look like. Ask your teacher for good examples of work by former pupils.*

Conclusion

- Your essay needs to embody a sense of finality. This should be reflected in the tone of your conclusion.
- Conclude by summing up your arguments and findings.
- It may be that you have found an alternative way of understanding the question.
- Maybe you will have discovered something that needs more research.
- It is important to explain what you learned from writing your essay. Give your views on the text(s) that you are writing about.

Two tips for writing better essays

Read outstanding exemplars

Ask your teacher whether he or she has exemplar essays for you to read. When you read the essays look especially for the following:

- how the essay's main argument is treated in the opening paragraph and developed throughout the rest of the essay.
- how the writer keeps the introduction brief by getting into the answer relatively quickly.
- how the writer maintains relevance by referring to key words and phrases from the essay title right from the beginning.
- how quotations (evidence) are introduced and commented on, where appropriate.
- how effectively the essay is concluded.

Mark other students' essays

Ask your teacher to photocopy your exam boards marking scheme so you can apply the exam board's criteria to your friends' essays.

Make sure you understand these terms before moving on!

- quotations
- historical context

QUICK TEST

1. What should you focus on in essay questions?
2. What does 'text' mean?
3. What does a text's 'historical context' mean?
4. How many main arguments should you aim for?
5. Where do you give your personal opinion in an essay?

Film extract assignment

Media coursework

Media studies can be examined either through coursework or exam. The following pages will help with coursework.

How you are graded

You will be assessed on your ability to analyse, review and comment on media texts using appropriate media terms. This assignment is graded for writing (EN3). Aim for the following:

- express complex ideas clearly, logically and persuasively
- show that you can make fine distinctions between points
- analyse (unravel) points in texts as you discuss them
- make sustained and detailed points
- use a wide range of grammatical constructions accurately
- be elaborate or concise, vigorous or restrained according to your purpose and audience
- show shape and control over your writing
- apply appropriate media terms effectively for your chosen text
- express clear personal interpretations.

Examples of set tasks

Media texts can include: advertisements, articles, scripts for film, television and radio, and any printed material published by the media. The following tasks are commonly set tasks:

- an examination of a news event and an analysis of attitudes and bias in the way the news event is reported in different sections of the media such as television, radio and newspapers
- an analysis of the opening of a film trailer or a brief extract from a film
- a written account of a practical activity in which you explain how you made a film, radio interview/show, or produced the front page for a newspaper
- an analysis of an advertisement from a magazine or newspaper

Over the next few pages you can study five sections on film grammar that will enable you to analyse an extract from a film. An essay plan and paragraph structure follows on page 43.

Film grammar 1

Lighting

Lighting helps create mood and atmosphere in film scenes (*A scene is a series of related shots and takes place in one time, action or location*). It encourages audiences to interpret what they see in a particular way. For instance, a fully lit scene creates a bright, non-threatening atmosphere. This compliments open and sometimes humorous dialogue; whereas scenes shot at night or with dark shadows often imply something menacing where a character is threatened, injured or worse.

There are three main types of lighting used on film sets:

- key lights: this is the main source of illumination on a set and it determines the general level and pattern of brightness

- backlights: at the back of the set to add depth or highlights
- filler lights: these help remove any unwanted shadows or contrasts created by the key light.

Directors can create a range of effects by switching off or manipulating these lights. Two good terms to use when analysing extracts from films are high-key lighting and low-key lighting. When the scene is fully lit it is the former and when lights are turned low or off it is the latter.

🌐 INTERNET

For more on lighting visit this website:

http://www.aber.ac.uk/media/Documents/short/gramtv.html

Film grammar 2

Colour

Colour This can also set the mood within scenes. Colours can reveal characters' personality, feelings and emotions and they can help signify a film's themes and ideas. Several directors use colour to set a tone within their films.

Colours carry with them **connotations** in which meanings are associated with each colour. Directors use colours to symbolically represent ideas in scenes for particular purposes. For example, green can represent jealousy, life, growth, triumph, etc.

Sound

Sound is crucial for making a film believable and for creating mood and meaning. Dialogue and sound effects enable audiences to make sense of what is happening, helping to create the feeling of being present at the action.

The following are the main types of sound used in films:

Diegetic sound (this means realistic sounds within the film's world).
These are the realistic sounds you expect to hear as you watch the visuals. These include: dialogue, the sound of a radio (if it is being played), footsteps, telephones ringing, doors closing, etc.

Non-diegetic sound: (sound added to the film's world)
This is sound added in the studio during editing. It includes: background music, voiceovers, sudden sounds added for special effects, any types of amplified sound, etc.

Sound bridges:

These are created through dialogue, music or other sound effects that begin from the next scene even though the present scene is not concluded. Sound bridges help give a sense of continuity by making a smooth transition between scenes.

Silence:

Directors sometimes use no sound at all to create a dramatic or tense atmosphere just before something threatening or sinister happens.

Mise-en-scène

Mise-en-scène is French and literally means 'put on stage'. In films it means 'everything that you can see in the frame or scene.' Everything that you see in a film scene is carefully selected to create an atmosphere, reveal a character and build upon audiences' expectations that arise out of film's genre.

The following should be noticed to appreciate mise-en-scène:
- the characters' appearance
- costumes
- make-up
- hairstyles
- acting styles
- props
- facial expressions and body language
- lighting and colour
- the setting
- the positioning of characters and objects
- camera distances and angles.

KEY TERMS

Make sure you understand these terms before moving on!
- lighting
- colour
- connotations
- sound
- mise-en-scène

Film extract assignment

Film grammar 3

Camera shots and **angles**

The way camera shots are framed – for size, angle and distance – can have a direct bearing on the narrative and how the audience react to what they see.

Directors usually shoot scenes with several cameras and then select a wide variety of shots during editing to build the visual story. There are many different types of camera shot; here are some of the main ones:

- establishing shot or long shot (ES or LS). The subject is at a distance from the camera. This establishes the location and occasionally, the time too.

- Total shot (TS) – a head-to-toe shot, usually with the purpose of introducing significant characters in a scene.

- Medium shot (MS) – generally focuses on a character from the knees or waist up; its often used to show relationships between characters in scenes.

- Close-up (CU) – focuses on characters' feelings and emotions, showing facial expression in great detail. It can focus on significant objects, too.

- Extreme close-up (ECU) – focuses on part of the head, body or prop. It can highlight emotions such as anger, joy, fear, etc.

- Point of view (POV) – shows a scene from a character's point of view

  - High angle shot (HA) – looks down on a character and often makes them appear vulnerable. This can also be a point of view shot scene through the eyes of a more powerful character.

  - Low angle shot (LA) – looks up at a character or object to make them appear more powerful or threatening. This is also known as 'worm's eye view'.

  - Over the shoulder shot (OS) – usually a close up or mid shot over a character's shoulder. This helps an audience gain an intimate view of a conversation.

  - Reaction shots (RS) – often short close ups or mid shots to catch the reaction of a character to a speech or action. These shots give a feeling of human interaction and reality to a scene.

  - Two or three shots – two or more characters appearing in the same frame.

Combining camera shots and angles
Camera shots and angles can be **combined** for various effects especially if they include point of view shots. For instance you can have a low angle, point of view shot.

Film grammar 4

Camera movement

Just as camera shots are framed to help audiences interpret a film's narrative, so **camera movement** can direct an audience's attention to details or a particular viewpoint within a film.

In the early days of films, scenes were shot with only one or two cameras on fixed tripods, so 'reality' appeared in a rather two-dimensional way. Now, directors commonly use multiple cameras so audiences can see the action from a range of perspectives giving a more realistic, three-dimensional experience.

Movement type	How camera moves	Where is it used?
Tracking	The camera tracks forward or pulls back from a character or the action, often along fixed tracks.	This gives a sense of realism.
Tilt shot	The camera moves up and down from a fixed axis.	This is good for a range of shots, including profiling characters by looking them up and down.
Panning	The camera shot moves from side to side on a fixed axis.	It aids realism and is useful for showing location shots, documentary style conversation, etc.
Rolling shot	This shot moves diagonally, making the image seem unbalanced.	It can be used for a variety of effects such as showing characters feeling ill or disorientated, etc.
Dolly shots	Camera moves on wheels to prevent camera wobble.	These can be a very versatile way of keeping up with the action. The shot combined with a zoomed-lens close up gives the feel, texture and characteristics of the subject as the camera moves alongside.
Crane shot	The camera is mounted on a crane well above the action.	It helps give a bird's-eye view. Characters can sometimes seem vulnerable, particularly to the elements such as the sea, weather, etc. Spot this shot in *Castaway*, starring Tom Hanks from 2001.

🌐 INTERNET

For more information on camera movement and camera shots, visit this website.

It has tables of cartoon images that will help you understand these terms very easily:

http://www.aber.ac.uk/media/Documents/short/gramtv.html

Make sure you understand these terms before moving on!

KEY TERMS

- camera shots
- camera angles
- combining camera shots and angles
- camera movement

Film extract assignment

Film grammar 5

Why edit a film?

Film directors and editors splice scenes together to form the most effective narrative for their films. Unused film footage of scenes and takes sometimes ends up as out-takes.

How does editing help a film's continuity?

The cuts should help the continuity (flow) of a film's storyline(s). The types of cuts directors insert can act as cues for audiences, helping them to pick up storylines quickly and easily.

Use the chart below to help you spot the most common types of edits in films.

Type of cut/edit	What it looks like	Its purpose
Straight cut	Hardly noticeable – it's like an eye-blink!	This is the most common type of cut and it normally borders long takes (long holding shots). This cut maintains narrative flow and helps create a sense of realism by hardly being noticed.
Dissolve	One image appears from beneath another.	The idea is to blend closely related scenes. This cut can also show a lapse of time or begin and end characters' flashbacks. It can also be used to create a creepy atmosphere.
Fade in/out	The screen darkens or lightens before the next image (and scene) fills the screen.	Often indicates a movement in time, a new location or another story within the main narrative. Fades can also indicate the end of an episode in a film.
Wipe cut	A new scene is introduced by one part of screen wiping away the old scene.	This cut often features in comedies or light-hearted action-adventure films to introduce new locations or storylines.
Jump cut	The camera shot jumps within a scene to someone or something.	These cuts make audiences focus suddenly on characters or props.
Montage	A number of brief shots follow in quick succession.	A montage can give a great deal of information in a brief period of time.

Special effects

Find out about how special effects such as computer generated graphics (CGI) and 'Blue-screen' are used in films because you may be able to include comments about them in your essays. *Remember that directors can speed up or slow down their scenes to create particular effects **(fast and slow motion)**.*

 INTERNET

Here are two excellent websites that should help with film grammar:

http://www.mediaknowall.com/filmlang.html

http://www.filmsite.org/filmterms1.html

Essay suggestion, plan and paragraph plan

Choosing your scene

Choose either an action-adventure or a thriller and select a three-minute or so sequence that is one of the following conventions (scenes expected in such movies):

- An action sequence (a major battle, natural disaster, etc.)
- A chase scene   ■ A fight scene
- A major stunt scene

Frame your question

Try to include the word 'how' as this will help you analyse your chosen film text. Here's an example of a likely essay title

How does the director,_____ _____ , create and maintain suspense in the central stunt/chase/ fight/action scene of _____? (Give the film's full title (19??/200? Give the year of the film.)

Planning and making notes for your essay

Analyse the sequence by making notes on how the director has constructed the scene with film language. View the scene five times and make notes each time on ONE of the points below:

- **Stunts and special effects**
- **Lighting and colour**
- **Sound**
- **Camera shots and angles**
- **Camera movement**
- **Mise-en-scène**
- **Editing**

Writing the essay

Work your way through each point. Select your best points because there is no need to say everything. For clarity introduce each paragraph with a topic sentence to signpost your arguments. Examples of sentence starters are available on this page. Add extra paragraphs if you need them.

Paragraph 1 (Introduction)

Keep your introduction brief. Identify the main convention of the sequence or scene. Is it an action/fight/chase/stunt scene? Introduce the main characters and give a short summary of what happens in the sequence or scene.

'_____' is an action-adventure/thriller featuring _____ This sequence/scene is a _____ scene. (Give the convention) and it features _____ _____

Paragraph 2 (Stunts and special effects)

The director's use of special effects is particularly striking in this scene. For instance, ...

Paragraph 3 (Lighting and colour)

Lighting and colour help create the scene's mood and atmosphere. For example, the director, ____ _____, uses _____ ...

Paragraph 4 (Sound)

The director's use of sound is crucial for the scene's suspense. For instance, the use of ...

Paragraph 5 (Camera shots)

Camera shots are important for the scene's suspense. For instance, as ...

Paragraph 6 (Camera movement)

The moving camera is important for various parts of the chase scene. For instance, the director uses a ... This produces the effect of ... and it helps maintain suspense during this sequence.

Paragraph 7 (Mise en scène)

There is no need here to repeat points on lighting and colour.
The director's use of props and location enhances the suspense because ...

Paragraph 8 (Editing)

The sequence uses ... to keep the audience in suspense ... For instance, there is ...

Paragraph 9 (Concluding your essay)

Conclude by stating how effectively the director has constructed the scene to maintain suspense, etc. Point out the scene's purpose for the audience and explain what you learned from working on this topic.

Make sure you understand these terms before moving on!

- stunts and special effects
- camera shots and angles
- camera movement
- editing

Practice questions

Use the questions to test your progress. Check your answers on page 93-94.

Original writing

1. Will you be assessed on writing or reading?
    ....

2. What is the word length that you should be aiming at?
    ....

3. What does 'narrative' mean?
    ....

4. What does 'genre' mean?
    ....

5. Similes are comparisons. How do they differ from metaphors?
    ....

6. What does 'hook' mean in terms of stories?
    ....

7. What is meant by 'setting'?
    ....

8. Give two examples of what you could write about as an assignment.
    ....

9. What does 'original writing' mean?
    ....

10. What are the main styles of narration?
    ....

11. If a narrator is outside the story, what is he or she?
    ....

12. What does 'plot' mean?
    ....

13. Give a method by which you can plan your story.
    ....

14. Explain what is meant by 'control' in writing.
    ....

15. If writing is linear what is it?
    ....

Non-fiction writing

16. What does non-fiction mean?
    ....

17. Give two examples of what you could write about.
    ....

18. If your task is 'discursive', how is it written?
    ....

19. Give three sources where you could find information on a topic.
    ....

20. Will an imaginative story be suitable for a non-fiction assignment?
    ....

21. What does 'target audience' mean?
    ....

22. Identify three forms that you could use for persuasive writing.

23. What is meant by the term 'text'?

24. Name a text that 'informs' or 'advises'.

25. Is biography a form of non-fiction?

26. If you are asked to 'compare' and 'contrast' what are you expected to do?

27. What is meant by the 'historical context' of a text?

28. Briefly explain what you need to do to write an essay.

29. Where do you put your personal views in an essay?

30. Explain what 'Point–Evidence–Comment' means.

Media coursework

31. What does lighting and colour help create in film scenes?

32. Give the term for lighting in which the scene is fully lit.

33. Give the two main terms for sound.

34. Why would a director use a sound bridge?

35. What does mise-en-scène literally mean?

36. Identify the following abbreviations for camera shots:
   - TS
   - ES
   - CU
   - MS
   - POV

37. Give the acronym for computer-generated graphics

38. What happens in a tracking shot?

39. In editing what is the commonest cut?

40. How would you recognise a montage?

How well did you do? 0–10 Try again 11–20 Getting there 21–30 Good work 31–40 Excellent!

45

Shakespeare assignment

What you may study

This will be determined by what your English teachers have in their stock cupboard; you'll probably get to study what Year 9 have not been set for their Sats! If you are lucky there will be a recent film of the play that you can rent which will help your overall understanding of it.

As you read the play try to get the gist of what characters are saying before you read passages again for a more detailed understanding. Make use of any general notes in your books to guide your understanding as well.

The plays you are most likely to study are:

Antony and Cleopatra   Macbeth ⌡
Henry IV Part One or Two   A Midsummer Night's Dream
Henry V   The Tempest ✓
Julius Caesar   Twelfth Night
The Merchant of Venice   The Winter's Tale
Romeo and Juliet ✓

How you will be graded

To achieve grades C to A* you will need to show that you are able to do some of the following.
1. You will show through your critical and personal response how meaning is made in the play.
2. You will be expected to support your points with textual evidence on the play's language, themes, characters or structure.
3. You should show that you understand the play and the implications from its themes and relevance for what people thought important in Shakespeare's day and in our time. Interpretations of texts can change over time as people read them in accordance with the values and ideas of their time.
4. In some of your comments you should show an awareness of Shakespeare's linguistic devices: his use of imagery through metaphors, similes, personification, alliteration, oxymorons, etc.
5. Try to say something about the play's **philosophical context** and how the play sits within its dramatic genre. The philosophical context means the values and ideas that were thought important when the play was written. An hour or two with an up-to-date history book of the time would help you find these things out.
6. You should give detailed and sustained analysis of Shakespeare's use of language for poetic, figurative, and dramatic effect and develop your points.
7. Try, if you can, to show an awareness of **alternative interpretations** in your writing.

What you have to do

You will need to show that you understand the play and can engage with it in an essay or through performance.

If your essay or writing or performance is going to be used to count for your Literature GCSE you'll also need to show an awareness of the background to the play. That is, the **historical, cultural and literary traditions** which shaped Shakespeare's play. Try to integrate this information in the extended comments that you use as evidence in your essays.

The Shakespeare Task

These days the best essay questions examine a play's characters, imagery, language, themes or structure by focusing on parts of scenes, whole scenes or whole acts rather than writing about the whole play. The new approach leads to better quality answers with more detailed comments on Shakespeare's characters and language. You can still show your knowledge of the whole play when writing on just a part of it. You could, for instance, be asked to compare a version of a particular scene with a version from a film or the theatre. Some teachers prefer students to perform a selected scene in a new time and setting so decisions can be made on how new audiences should interpret the characters, themes, imagery and language. This approach is always followed by the writing of a drama statement instead of an essay.

Shakespeare's choice of language

Shakespeare used three styles of writing in his plays. Here are a few examples from *Twelfth Night*:
1. **Rhyming couplets** Often used to signal the end of scenes like a curtain call or for heightened dramatic effect. Take, for example, this rhyming couplet from *Twelfth Night*:
   Duke Orsino: *Away before me to sweet beds of flowers:*
   Love-thoughts lie rich when canopied with bowers.
2. **Blank verse** (Unrhymed) Verse which was intended to represent the rhythms of speech. It is usually used by noble characters who are given elevated speech to show their feelings and mood:
   Duke Orsino: *If music be the food of love play on.*
   Note how the speech is in iambic pentameter. That is, it has 10 syllables to the line in which five are stressed. The rhythm pattern is ti-tum, ti-tum, ti-tum, ti-tum, ti-tum. Sometimes you'll find more or fewer stresses to the lines yet the overall pattern will be even in the end.

3. **Prose** Ordinary language used by characters of all ranks.
   Uneducated characters tend to use it. It can also be used for comic exchanges between characters, for plot development and for speech which lacks dramatic intensity:

   Viola as Cesario: *Save thee, friend, and thy music. Dost thou live by thy tabor?*
   Feste: *No, sir, I live by the church.*
   Viola: *Art thou a churchman?*
   Feste: *No such matter sir: I do live by the church; for I do live at my house, and my house doth stand by the church.*

Make sure you understand these terms before moving on!
- philosophical context
- alternative interpretations
- historical and literary traditions
- imagery ■ rhyming couplets
- blank verse ■ prose

QUICK TEST
1. Give an example of a Shakespeare assignment that you could do.
2. What is 'textual evidence'?
3. Why does Shakespeare use blank verse?
4. Why does Shakespeare use poetic verse?

Structure and themes

This typical structure or *plot* of a Shakespeare play is oversimplified, but this basic framework should help you see how the play that you are studying is set out.

Some recurring themes, ideas or messages

Conflict
Macbeth, Julius Caesar, Romeo and Juliet, Antony and Cleopatra, The Merchant of Venice, Henry IV Parts I and *II* and *Henry V.*

Various forms of love and loyalty
Twelfth Night, Romeo and Juliet, A Midsummer Night's Dream, The Merchant of Venice, Antony and Cleopatra and *The Winter's Tale.*

Change
Characters in most plays. Some characters such as Malvolio (*Twelfth Night*) and Shylock (The Merchant of Venice), are punished because they cannot change.

Fate
Most plays; also the role of the individual against society.

Fortune
Every play. This is the notion of the Goddess of Fortune making and breaking us by giving or denying us luck.

Order, Disorder and Stability
Most plays. This is usually linked to Nature.

Good and Evil
Most plays.

Appearance and Reality
Most comedies and some tragedies. The themes probably reflect the great changes in society during Shakespeare's time.

Disguise and Identity
Most comedies and some tragedies. The plays often depict the gap between what is said and how it is interpreted. Characters can deceitfully misuse words too.

Self-Knowledge
This can be found in most comedies; however there is often one character, like Malvolio in Twelfth Night, who is incapable of accepting his faults and learning about himself.

Kingship and the use and abuse of power
Macbeth, Julius Caesar, Henry IV Parts I and II and Henry V.

Justice
Several plays including The Merchant of Venice and Macbeth.

Love and Marriage
Several plays.

Plot structure

Shakespeare liked to stress the comedy or seriousness of many scenes within his plays by making **dramatic contrasts**. He did this by placing a serious scene after a comic one and vice versa.

- Main characters are introduced to the audience. Order reigns and the world and nature are in natural harmony.

- Problems are revealed. Things begin to go wrong. Confusions, murders, deceit, pranks and other complications begin.

- As events progress there is chaos and a loss of order and harmony. The natural world appears out of sorts.

- Things come to a head in the play's **climax**. ('Climax' comes from the Greek word for 'ladder'). If you are reading a tragedy then several more deaths occur now, including a main character like Macbeth. The climax is the moment of the highest dramatic intensity in the play, particularly for the main character.

- Order is re-established with the right people in control again. Nature is again at one with the main characters. Comedies usually end in several, sometimes three, marriages.

Always be prepared to say what you think of the play that you studied. Your view is important and it should be expressed at the end of your essay.

Go to see a live performance of a play, if you can, because this will help your understanding of the play. Shakespeare intended his plays to be performed and not read when he wrote them.

KEY TERMS

Make sure you understand these terms before moving on!
- climax
- dramatic contrasts
- plot
- themes

QUICK TEST

1. What is a theme?
2. Where would you find the 'climax' of a play?
3. What does 'plot' mean?
4. What does 'context' mean?
5. Why would it be useful to see a performance of a Shakespeare play?

Shakespeare's imagery

Figures of speech

Shakespeare uses figures of speech – that is, **imagery** or word pictures – to do the following:
- say more about points made in dialogue and action
- reinforce and enhance the audience's ideas of the characters
- magnify or draw attention to themes/issues in the text.

To do this he uses:
- **similes**: comparisons using 'as' or 'like':
  'The moon is like a balloon.'

- **personification**: giving human feelings to animals or inanimate objects.

- **metaphors**: stronger comparisons saying something is something else:
  'The moon is a balloon.'

- **motifs**: characters, themes or images which recur throughout a text. For example, disguise is a running idea in *Twelfth Night*. In *Macbeth* there are several motifs. One is 'fair and foul' and another is sleep. To the Weird Sisters, who characterise evil, what is ugly is beautiful, and what is beautiful is ugly: 'Fair is foul and foul is fair.' Macbeth and Lady Macbeth reign in restless ecstasy after murdering King Duncan. Macbeth soon says to illustrate the sleep motif:

  'Me thought I heard a voice cry, "Sleep no more!"
  Macbeth does murder sleep — the innocent sleep,
  Sleep that knits up the ravelled sleave of care,
  The death of each day's life, sore labour's bath,
  Balm of hurt minds, great nature's second course
  Chief nourisher in life's feast.'
  – *Macbeth, Act 2, Scene 2, 34–39*

- extended metaphors: a metaphor that is used extensively throughout a passage.

- **oxymorons**: these are words and phrases that you would not expect to see yoked together to cause an effect. As soon as Juliet hears that Tybalt, her cousin, has been killed by Romeo, her grief and outrage is tempered by her disbelief that Romeo could carry out such a deed:

  'Fiend angelical, dove-feathered raven, wolvish-ravening lamb,
  ... A damned saint, an honourable villain!'
  – *Romeo and Juliet, Act 3, Scene 2, lines 75–79*

> *If the audience knows more about a development of the plot than the characters then this is known as dramatic irony.*

> *Keep quotations relevant and brief. Aim to use single words and phrases or no more than a sentence or so to prove your points. Remember to comment on the quotations that you use: your style should be P.E.C. (point – evidence – comment).*

An extended example of Shakespeare's use of imagery

In the following speech from *King Lear*, Kent is enquiring of a Gentleman whether Cordelia, the daughter of King Lear, has been upset by a letter describing her father's condition.

Kent   O, then it mov'd her?
Gentleman Not to a rage. Patience and sorrow strove
            Who should express her goodliest. You have seen
            Sunshine and rain at once: her smiles and tears
            Were like a better way. Those happy smilets
            That play'd on her ripe lip seem'd not to know
            What guests were in her eyes, which parted thence
            As pearls from diamonds dropp'd. In brief,
            Sorrow would be a rarity most belov'd,
            If all could so become it.

The gentleman describes Cordelia's conflicting emotions in a number of ways.

He uses personification to make the struggle in her mind between patience and sorrow seem more vivid.

He then uses metaphors of 'sunshine' and 'rain' to express these emotions.

Personification is again used to give an impression of the strength of her emotions to characterise the 'smilets' (small smiles) that 'played' on her lips, and the tears that were 'guests' in her eyes.

He uses a simile to describe the richness and beauty of Cordelia's tears which part from her eyes *as pearls from diamonds dropp'd'.*

This moment is very moving and it is an example of Shakespeare's **dramatic technique**. He has Cordelia's reaction described rather than calling upon an actress to play it.

 Get a recording of a play from your local library and listen to parts of the play as it is read. It will help your understanding of the play.

KEY TERMS

- imagery
- similes
- personification
- metaphors
- motifs
- oxymorons
- dramatic technique

QUICK TEST

Circle the correct answer:

1. A theme is:
   a) a song b) an idea/issue or message c) personification
   d) a character.

2. Shakespeare uses imagery to:
   a) make his writing pretty b) because he is vain c) fill up space
   d) enhance our understanding of a character, theme or a point.

3. A simile is a figure of speech which:
   a) draws a comparison using 'as' or 'like' b) allows characters
   to smile c) has to do with singularity d) makes a comparison
   using 'is' or 'are'?

4. The term 'imagery' means:
   a) looking in mirrors b) word pictures c) writing prose d) knitting.

5. The climax of a play is:
   a) its ending b) its beginning c) when the action comes to a head
   d) in the middle.

An essay on Caliban

Introduction

The Tempest
On meeting Stephano and Trinculo Caliban learns the joys of drink. He sees them as gods come to save him from the slavery of Prospero. They plan to kill Prospero but a quarrel breaks out thanks to an invisible Ariel. Caliban's plot is reported to Prospero and comes to nothing.

Synopsis

Caliban is the son of the witch Sycorax and the **original inhabitant** of the island on which the play is set. As such he represents some aspects of Elizabethan ideas of **the noble savage**.

When Prospero arrived at the island he released Ariel from his captivity and attempted to 'civilise' Caliban. Unfortunately Caliban proved **unteachable** and attempted to rape Miranda – see Act 1 Scene 2. The more **sinister side** of Caliban's name is suggested by its similarity to '**cannibal**.'

Following his fall from grace Caliban works as a servant for Prospero but feels that the island has been stolen from him (Act 1 Scene 2)

Caliban is not without redeeming features. He is sensitive to the natural world of the island and entranced by the noises and music he hears. (Act 3 Scene 2)

Caliban's ugliness is constantly emphasised. Miranda calls him an 'abhorred slave' whilst Trinculo and Stephano refer to him as a 'moon-calf' and a 'monster'.

Although Caliban is **punished** for his plot against Prospero he is eventually

Caliban's role within the play

Although Caliban has some comic scenes with Trinculo and Stephano his encounters with Prospero reveal a sense of failure and powerlessness on the part of the magician. His attempts to educate Caliban have been repaid only with curses.

As the original inhabitant of the island Caliban represents all the native people encountered by Europeans in the Elizabethan era of exploration. Through Caliban Shakespeare explores the idea of the noble savage and questions the assumptions often made about them.

The play also explores the debate between **Nature and Nurture**. Caliban is evil in a way, but he has had none of the advantages of a European education. Antonio on the other hand is a sophisticated courtier who has had all the benefits of education and upbringing. Antonio, it turns out, is as inclined to evil and plotting as Caliban. To Antonio the island is nothing but a baron desert but to Caliban it is a place of enchantment.

Caliban's appearance

Miranda	'Tis a villain, sir, I do not love to look upon. (1, ii, 312)
Prospero	A freckled whelp hag-born – not honoured with A human shape. (1, ii,282)
Prospero	Thou poisonous slave, got by the devil himself Upon thy wicked dam. (1, ii, 321)
Trinculo	What have we here? A man or a fish? Dead or alive? A fish: he smells like a fish; a very ancient and fish like smell. A strange fish! Legg'd like a man! And his fins like arms! (2, ii, 25)
Stephano	Have we devils here? Do you put tricks upon's with salvages and men of Ind, ha? This is some monster of the isle... Where the devil did he learn our language?... An abominable monster! (2, ii, 58)

Caliban on:

Prospero

I must obey: his Art is of such pow'r
It would control my dam's god, Setebos,
And make a vassal of him. (I, 2)

All the infections that the sun sucks up
From bogs, fens, flats, on Prosper fall, and make
him
By inch-meal a disease! His spirits hear me...
For every trifle they are set upon me;
Sometimes like apes, that mow and chatter at me,
And after bite me; then like hedgehogs, which
Lie tumbling in my barefoot way, and mount
Their pricks at my footfall; sometime am I
All wound with adders, who with cloven tongues
Do hiss me into madness (II,2)

Miranda

You taught me language, and my profit on't
Is, I know how to curse. The red plague rid you
    For learning me your language! (I,2)

And that most deeply to consider is
The beauty of his daughter; he himself
Calls her a nonpareil. I never saw a woman
But only Sycorax my dam and she;
But she as far surpasseth Sycorax
As great'st does least. (III, 2)

Trinculo

That's a brave god, and bears celestial liquor. I
will kneel to him. I do adore thee. I'll show thee
every fertile inch of the island; and I will kiss thy
foot. I prithee, be my god. (III, 2)

'Ban, 'Ban, Ca-Caliban
Has a new master, get a new man! (III, 2)

The Island

Be not afeard. The isle is full of noises,

Sounds, and sweet airs, that give delight, and hurt
not.
Sometimes a thousand twangling instruments
Will hum about mine ears; and sometimes voices,
That, if I then had wak'd after long sleep,
Will make me sleep again; and then, in dreaming,
The clouds methought would open and show riches
Ready to drop upon me, that, when I wak'd,
I cried to dream again. (III, 2)

This island's mine, by Sycorax my mother,
Which thou tak'st from me. When thou came'st first,
Thou strok'st me, and made much of me; wouldst
give me
Water with berries in't; and teach me how
To name the bigger light, and how the less,
That burn by day and night: and then I lov'd thee,
And show'd thee all the qualities of the isle,
The fresh springs, brine-pits, barren place and fertile:
Curs'd be I that did so! (I, 2)

QUICK TEST

1. What are the main ways in which you can find out about a character?
2. Name the three main types of Shakespeare plays.
3. Why does Shakespeare have important characters speak soliloquies?

The Tempest: an essay plan

Planning an essay

Title: How does Shakespeare present Caliban in *The Tempest*? Is he a noble savage or just a savage? The three steps in planning this essay are.

- Read the question carefully and identify the key words.
- Review the notes on the previous page.
- Decide which material is relevant and how you are going to structure them.

Plan your essay along the following lines:

Introduction – response to question and issues involved.

Section 1
Arguments in favour of the idea that Caliban is just a savage
- Poor response to education
- Attempt to rape Miranda
- **Hatred and fear** of Prospero
- Response to alcohol
- Attitude to Trinculo – treats him as god
- Attempt to overthrow Prospero

Section 2
Arguments in favour of noble savage idea
- He is the original inhabitant of the island dispossessed by Prospero.
- His **sensitivity** to the island
- 'Isle is full of noises' speech – sensitive nature
- **Self awareness** shown when cursing Miranda for teaching him to speak
- Compare his behaviour with Trinculo, Stephano and Antonio

Section 3
Significance of Caliban's ugliness
- Surface only?
- Prejudice?
- Compare Antonio's rich clothes hiding deeper sin

Section 4
Shakespeare's presentation – how the audience's sympathies are manipulated
- Introduced as servant
- History explained in Act 1 Scene 2 – early innocent response turns sour
- **Sympathy** for him because he is ruled by fear?
- Meeting with Trinculo and Stephano – comedy. Do we lose or gain sympathy when he chooses Trinculo as his new master?
- His **innocence/ignorance** – only seen two women – compare Miranda's 'O brave new world'
- Punishment by Ariel – is this excessive?
- Plot revealed – was he ever really a danger?

Shakespeare's language and theatrical techniques
- Caliban's curses – close analysis
- More poetic speeches – close analysis
- Costume issues. Compare Ariel.

Conclusion
- No easy answer – Caliban both noble and savage
- Why you think Shakespeare doesn't make simple choice
- Personal opinion

Once you have planned your essay you need to go back to the text to find suitable quotations and references. Post-it notes inserted in the book are a good idea at this stage.

Refining your argument

The introduction

Your opening paragraph should address the key points of the question. The most important word is 'present' as it asks you not simply to discuss whether Caliban is a savage, but to talk about how Shakespeare introduces and manipulates these ideas. You can also at this point explain that the issue of noble savages would have been interesting to an Elizabethan audience living in an age of exploration.

The body of the essay should:

- be well supported by **quotation** and close references

- avoid retelling the story of the play

- comment on each part of the story in terms of its affect on **audience sympathy**

Conclusion

You do not need to restate the whole argument but you should think in terms of what you have learned from writing the essay. Consider:

- What the balance between 'noble' and 'savage' is.

- Why Shakespeare made a minor character like Caliban so bad and so good.

For improved expression in your arguments look at the linking words and phrases section on pages 20–21 to help you signpost your argument. Try to link your ideas together and make connections between your points wherever you can.

INTERNET

Web sites for help with Shakespeare plays

Mr. William Shakespeare and the Internet:

http://shakespeare.palomar.edu/

Another good one with some study guides is

Absolute Shakespeare:

http://absoluteshakespeare.com/index.htm

Make sure you understand these terms before moving on!

- hatred and fear
- sensitivity
- self awareness
- sympathy
- innocence/ignorance
- quotation
- audience sympathy

Sample opening paragraph

Caliban in *The Tempest* is both a Savage and a Noble Savage. At first sight he seems to be a monster and a source of trouble within the play, but Shakespeare also presents Caliban sympathetically as the displaced original inhabitant of the island. Through Caliban Shakespeare explores important ideas to do with the nature of evil, the morality of colonisation and the idea of the Noble Savage.

Notice that this introduction indicates the main areas that you will deal with in the essay.

Essay spidergrams

Re-read your text

Whether you are reading a play, novel or short story, you must re-read your text for a deeper understanding of your essay question or task. Many teachers concentrate on scenes from plays and chapters from novels for written assignments. In plays they expect pupils to focus on **dramatic technique**. For example, you may be asked to show how **dramatic tension** is created in a particular scene. In novels you might be expected to show how a **theme**,

character, **imagery** or **mood**, has been represented. One of the best ways of making notes for your essay is to produce a memorable spidergram. Study your essay question or task and try to build up relevant comments by looking carefully at key words and phrases in your question.

When to use a spidergram

If your essay title asks you to write about a character, theme or any aspect of a text that you are studying, you could do a spidergram like the one on the opposite page. Study your essay question and try to build up relevant comments by looking carefully at key words and phrases in your question. Check your ideas again by rereading key parts of the text.

 The habit of producing spidergrams or brainstorms that focus on three or four main points will help you plan your answers when you take the final exams.

Study the characters

You can learn about characters by examining:
- what they say
- what they do
- what other characters say about them
- stage directions
- how they develop (that is, do they change or do they remain the same? If so, why?)

Build your spidergram as you read

Go through the play or text and look at the places where your character speaks or others speak about him/her. Build your spidergram up gradually as you do so.

1   Use white paper without lines – it helps you think more clearly.
2   Use a pencil and a rubber – it is quicker and you can add colours, too.
3   Begin in the middle of the page with a title (this could be the name of a character or a theme) and put the most important information around the title.
4   Work your way out to the margins where you should put the least important information.
5   Your first five minutes are likely to be the most productive so do not stop for anything. You can make your map pretty and memorable afterwards.
6   Remember that the colours you choose for various topics of your spidergram can be meaningful because everything can be given an appropriate colour. Colours can also act as prompts to help you recall ideas.
7   You can make connections between ideas by running branches off your main ideas. Draw connecting branches to other main ideas if it seems sensible. Your spidergram will then take on the character of a colourful tube map; you can then add appropriate pictures and images.
8   Remember that pictures will bring ideas to life as well as help you remember them. If you are hopeless at drawing simply cut likely pictures out of magazines.
9   Keep spidergrams to one piece of paper. If you run out of space, tape another sheet of paper on to the side of the paper where you are running out of space. It does not matter how big your piece of paper is as long as it is one side of paper. You can always carefully fold it up afterwards.

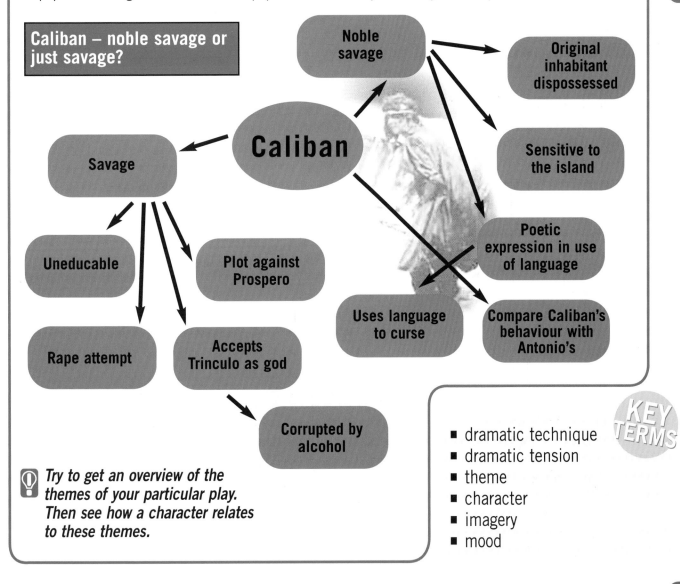

Caliban – noble savage or just savage?

Noble savage

Original inhabitant dispossessed

Caliban

Savage

Sensitive to the island

Uneducable

Plot against Prospero

Poetic expression in use of language

Uses language to curse

Compare Caliban's behaviour with Antonio's

Rape attempt

Accepts Trinculo as god

Corrupted by alcohol

💡 *Try to get an overview of the themes of your particular play. Then see how a character relates to these themes.*

KEY TERMS

- dramatic technique
- dramatic tension
- theme
- character
- imagery
- mood

Practice questions

Use the questions to test your progress. Check your answers on page 94.

Shakespeare assignment

1. Name two plays you may study.

   ....

2. Briefly explain a method of understanding passages from Shakespeare.

   ....

3. Identify two types of assignments that you could produce on a Shakespeare play.

   ....

4. What does 'textual evidence' mean?

   ....

5. Can the interpretation of a Shakespeare play change over time?

   ....

6. If so, why?

   ....

7. What does 'linguistic devices' mean?

   ....

8. What are the main genres of Shakespeare plays?

   ....

9. What does 'philosophical context' mean?

   ....

10. List the three styles of writing Shakespeare used in his plays.

    ....

11. Why did Shakespeare use rhyming couplets?

    ....

12. What is the purpose of blank verse?

    ....

Structure and themes

13. What does Shakespeare like to establish at the beginning of his plays?

    ....

14. What happens next?

    ....

15. What is the 'climax' of a play?

    ....

16. What could happen during the 'climax' of a play?

    ....

17. Briefly explain what usually happens at the end of a Shakespeare play.

    ....

18. What is a 'theme'?

    ....

19. Identify three themes that can be found in Shakespeare's plays.

....

20. What type of themes might you expect to find in a comedy?

....

21. Briefly explain what is meant by 'dramatic contrast'.

....

22. Why did Shakespeare build dramatic contrasts into his plays?

....

23. Explain what is meant by 'self-knowledge'.

....

24. Briefly sum up the typical structure of a Shakespeare play.

....

Imagery and essay plans

25. What is meant by the term 'figures of speech'?

....

26. What is a simile?

....

27. Why is a metaphor a stronger comparison?

....

28. What is an extended metaphor?

....

29. What is meant by personification?

....

30. Define an oxymoron.

....

31. What is a motif?

....

32. Give two reasons why Shakespeare uses imagery in his plays.

....

33. Shakespeare uses a great deal of irony in his plays. What is irony?

....

34. What is dramatic irony?

....

35. Why and where would you expect to find passages rich in imagery?

....

36. Briefly sum up what is meant by imagery.

....

How well did you do?   X   0–9 Try again   10–18 Getting there   11–27 Good work   28–36 Excellent! ✓

59

Reading set poems

What you have to study

- Poetry is a significant part of your GCSE English and GCSE English Literature courses.
  In English you will study some poetry. Usually it will be modern and in some boards it will relate to a work on different cultures. It may be assessed either through exam or coursework depending on the options your teacher has chosen.

- In English Literature you must study a variety of poems from the English literary heritage. In most cases poetry is assessed through the examination rather than coursework and is chosen either from an exam board anthology or a set poetry text.

- None of the boards will ask you to comment on poetry that you have not seen before and in no case will you have to write about a single poem; you will alway have the opportunity to compare and contrast different poems.

- The type of poems that you will study will range from **ballads** (narrative or story poems) to **sonnets** (serious poems that explore deep themes such as love and death) and you will be expected to make connections between them on the basis of content, theme and technique.

> *Do not merely identify figures of speech and other poetic techniques, show how they affect meaning in your poem.*

Reading a poem

Aim to read the poems at least three times and do the following very carefully.

- Explain briefly what you think the poem is about. You are looking for an overview at this stage. This early view of the poem may change once you have studied it in greater detail.

- Examine how the poet gets their meaning across to us through their choice of form, language, imagery and themes. You will also need to consider the poem's **tone**. For instance, what is the attitude of the speaker towards the topic or theme? What is their attitude to you? Does the poem's tone change in the poem? Go through each area as fully as you can.

DUFFY...
HUGHES...
PLATH...
RUMENS...
ADCOCK...

- Explain your views again on the poem, stating what the poem is about. Point out what can be learned from the poem, including any changes of mind you may have had after working through the first two points given above.

Writing about poems

You are unlikely to be asked to write about a single poem – you will need to compare and contrast. You can compare:

- Narratives (where present)
- Ideas
- Themes
- Imagery and other literary devices
- Language choice
- Verse form
- Rhythm

If you are given a choice of poems to compare make sure you choose poems that have similarities or interesting differences in several of these areas.

How you will be graded

To achieve grades C to A star you will need to:

- show that you have engaged with the poems by giving a sustained and developed response to key words and phrases in your essay question. More sophisticated answers will display an enthusiastic personal response with close textual analysis

- explore the poems and show insight. Again, more sophisticated responses will show greater insight or exploration of the poems

- identify the verse form and explain how its genre contributes towards the poem's meaning

- explain how the poet has used language and imagery in the poem. In other words, you will need to be able to identify word choices (**diction**) and what they may suggest as well as show how the poet uses figures of speech, such as similes, to add meaning to their ideas and messages in their poems. More developed responses will show how the poet uses similar themes or points and ideas in several poems. Such responses will also point out similarities or contrasts in the poet's use of language, form and other aspects of poetic technique

- say something about the poet's purposes and intentions. What is the poet setting out to achieve?

- identify with the poet's intentions or the view of the **narrator** in the poem. In other words, show empathy

- give a sophisticated response that is convincing and imaginative, showing a high degree of empathy

- display analytical and interpretive skills when examining the social, moral and philosophical significance of the poems.

KEY TERMS

- ballads
- sonnets
- tone
- diction
- narrator

QUICK TEST

1. How much of your final mark is your work on poetry likely to be worth?
2. What kind of poem is a ballad?
3. Where would you write your personal views in an exam essay?
4. How many times should you read a poem?
5. What is empathy?

Writing about poetry (EN2)

Tips on writing about poetry

One of the biggest problems in writing about poetry is finding **phrases** that enable you to express your ideas and make your writing **flow**. This framework is not really meant as a substitute for your **structure**, just a helping hand in case you get stuck. You should aim to integrate useful phrases into your writing so that you can explain yourself with ease in exams. Beware, however, of always using the same phrases, which would lead to a mechanical style.

- Introduce points that you want to make by using some of the phrases given below; change them around, or simply add them together. The more fluent you are the more impressive your points will be.

- Good grades in exams are achieved through knowing your texts and being able to express your points in a fluent manner. You will also be judged on your **punctuation**, your use of **standard English** and the quality of your **expression**.

- Look out for useful ways of expressing your ideas and making a note of them. Successful pupils are able to make their points in essays in a fluent and knowledgeable manner.

Sample poems

The Eagle
He clasps the crag with crooked hands;
Close to the sun in lonely lands,
Ring'd with the azure world, he stands.
The wrinkled sea beneath him crawls;
He watches from his mountain walls,
And like a thunderbolt he falls.

Alfred Tennyson

A Song
Lying is an occupation
used by all who mean to rise:
Politicians owe their station
But to well-concerted lies.

These to lovers give assistance
To ensnare the fair one's heart;
And the virgin's best resistance
Yields to this commanding art.

Study this superior science,
Would you rise in church or state;
Bid to truth a bold defiance,
'Tis the practise of the great.

Laetitia Pilkington (1708–50)

1. Introductory phrases

- The poem … is/seems to be about …

- The poem is narrated in the first/second person.
  This aids/enhances the poem's meaning as/because …

- The form of the poem is (a ballad/sonnet/two-, three-, four-, five-line stanzas/free verse) … This is an appropriate form for the poem because it helps readers appreciate …

2. Phrases for the middle of a piece of writing

- The theme/idea of ... is present/repeated in both poems.

- For instance ... . The poet contrasts ... with ... .

- The poet uses appropriate language/diction to convey a feeling of ... . For instance ...

- The caesura after ... helps an audience understand ... .

- The use of alliteration/assonance/onomatopoeia with ... shows ... .

- The poet's use of imagery (similes/metaphors/personification) can be seen with ... . This shows/intensifies the idea of ... .

- Another interesting example of this is ... . This emphasises/shows/reinforces/gives a sense of/refers to ... .

- The poem's meaning is enhanced/deepened with ...

- An example of which is ... . This refers to the main idea of ... .

- For example, this can be seen with ... .

- The poem reflects the narrator's/poet's feelings on/of ... .

- The poet reminds the reader of ... with ... .

- The poet draws attention to the fact that ... .

- The poet compares ... with ... .

> **It is important to be precise when writing about poetry. Remember that 'verse' means the whole poem or a collection of poems. You should use 'stanza' when you want to describe a part of a poem, such as a four-line 'quatrain'.**

3. Phrases to sum up your arguments and views

- The poem's/narrator's tone is one of ... . This helps the reader/audience appreciate the/how ...

- The tone(s) in each poem is/are ... . This/these show(s) ...

- To sum up I would say that the poet feels ... about his/her subject. The poet wants us to understand/feel the ...

- Both/each of the poems show ... . This shows the poet's feelings of ...

- From reading these poems I learned that ...

- My final view of the poem (s) is that it is/they are ...

Make sure you understand these terms before moving on!

- phrases
- flow
- structure
- punctuation
- standard English
- expression

QUICK TEST

1. Find out what the term 'caesura' means.
2. Find out the number of lines in a sonnet.
3. What is alliteration?
4. What is a writing frame?

Comparing poems

Writing about poetry

Writing about poetry for either coursework or for exams will allow you to show your ability to compare and contrast different texts. Poems are usually grouped by author, theme or some aspect of poetic technique.

When studying works by the **same author** remember to look out for:

- Consistent themes across poems
- Particular points of view the poet adopts
- Typical subject matter
- Poetic techniques that the poet favours

For instance:

Seamus Heaney, is an Irish poet who frequently writes about nature. His poems are often autobiographical and some are tinged with nostalgia. He uses a variety of verse forms but his language is usually simple and direct.

If you are looking at poems that have been grouped by **theme** remember to look out for:

- Similarities in the approaches the authors have taken to the theme
- Differences between the authors' approaches
- Similarities and differences in the way that authors have used language to express their ideas
- Similarities and differences in the way that authors have used poetic techniques

Choosing poems

If you are writing about poetry you will have a wide range of poems to choose from but most exam questions give you the name of at least one poem and ask you to choose another similar poem.

It is very important to choose the right poem at this stage and you are likely to have to spend some time in your exam preparation classes grouping poems together by subject matter, theme and technique. Ask yourself:

- Does my second poem have enough in common with the first?
- Are there enough significant differences?

If the poems have little in common your essay will be difficult to write.
If the poems are too similar your essay will probably be rather flat and uninteresting.

Approaching poems

It is a good idea to begin your discussion of any poem with a simple statement of what you think it is about. When you are comparing poems this is even more important, as it allows you state similarities and differences at an early stage. For instance, you could begin a comparison of Jenny Joseph's poem *Warning* and Seamus Heaney's *Follower*:

> Both these poems are about growing old. Jenny Joseph looks forward to her own old age when she can be less responsible than she is now, whereas Seamus Heaney is saddened by the decline of his father into old age.

What to compare

To gain a good grade you will need to focus not only on the ideas and opinions in the poems but also on their **poetic technique** (often referred to as the **language** of the poem.) You will either have a copy of the poem printed in the exam paper or you will be working on a examination anthology. It is essential that you pay close attention to detail and make extensive use of quotation.

You will be looking for:

- Striking or unusual word choice
- Use of metaphor, simile, personification and other literary devices
- Use of sounds in rhyme, alliteration and onomatopoeia
- Use of rhythm in choice of long and short words etc
- Use of verse form such as ballad metre, sonnet, free verse

Answering the question

A typical higher tier poetry question might be:

> Look again at *Wind* by Ted Hughes and at least one other poem from the Nature section of your anthology and show how the words used create powerful imagery involving sight, sound or movement.
>
> In your answer you should make close reference to the language.

The first thing to do is to look closely at the named poem. As you do so, think about other poems that you have studied and try to think of one that is a good match in terms of the key words of the question. When you have chosen the second poem you can begin thinking of points of similarity and difference.

Remember at this stage that you can make notes on the question paper or in the anthology – underline and circle words which you think are relevant to the question so that you can use them as supporting quotation in your essay.

Make sure you understand these terms before moving on!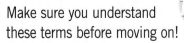

- same author
- theme
- poetic technique
- language

Planning a poetry essay

Planning your essay

A question on the **theme** of childhood might be:

What views of childhood do the poets create, and how do they do this, in two of the following poems?

Growing Up (Fanthorpe)

Follower (Heaney)

I remember, I remember (Larkin)

Remember to refer closely to words and images from the poems to support your answer.

To answer this question need to plan your essay carefully based on the poems you have chosen and the **key words** you have identified in the question.

Make a table like the one below to help you to make comparisons.

	Childhood			
	views of childhood poets create	how they do this	words and imagery from the poems	Poetic technique (verse form, rhyme, etc.)
Follower				
I remember, I remember				

Notice that the heading in the first three columns are taken directly from the question.

Do this planning in your exam answer booklet – take up as much space as you need.

You can use a whole page of your exam booklet if you wish.

If you use a large table to make notes you should be able to fill it in with details and references to the poems. Alternatively you could use a spider diagram.

Organising your essay

There are two main ways to organise your comparisons of the poems. These are:

- Write about poem one; write about poem two; draw comparisons between them
- Write about theme of poem one; write about theme of poem two; compare themes; then go on to language and imagery of poem one; and so on.

The first method is straightforward but it can involve some repetition at the comparison stage.

The second method takes planning and is slightly more complicated.

Remember however, you gain most marks for comparing the poems – if you leave the comparison to the end there is a danger that you might run out of time for this important task.

Effective openings

Every year examiners comment that students spending too much valuable exam time 'writing in'. This means general writing at the beginning of an answer that does actually address the question. To avoid this you need to give a moment's thought to how to start your essay.

To answer to the question on the previous page you need to do three things.

■ Tell the examiner which poems you will be writing about.

■ Show why you have chosen your second poem.

■ Give some idea of what the main similarities and differences are.
This should take three or four lines at most. For instance:

| Poems identified | | Points out a significant area of similarity |

I remember, I remember by Philip Larkin and *Follower* by Seamus Heaney both feature a man looking back on his childhood. However, the two poems show very different attitudes to that time; Heaney remembers his early days with great clarity and vigour, whereas Larkin's poem is more concerned with what he can not remember.

| How the poems are related to the themes | | Points out a significant area of difference. |

Compare and contrast

In making comparisons you might find the following pronouns and connectives useful.

As with other writing use **PEC** – Point, Example, Comment.
For instance:
Neither poet paints a very flattering portrait of himself.(P)
Heaney says 'I stumbled in his hobnailed wake' (E) as if his father was a great ship cutting through the soil and was just a nuisance following behind (C). In contrast to this Larkin seems to be imagining an eventful childhood for himself but even here he uses the very negative word (C) 'doggerel' (E) to describes his youthful verse.

Comparing	Contrasting
each	neither
both	but
similarly	however
equally	differently
likewise	on the other hand
in comparison	in contrast
in the same way	conversely

Conclusion

When you have completed your discussion of the poems try to draw a general conclusion. Words and phrases like 'to sum up' or 'In conclusion' or 'finally' can be used at this stage. You should try to give an overall impression of what you have said. For instance:

In conclusion neither Larkin nor Heaney had what could be called an 'exciting' childhood but to Heaney his very ordinary father seemed strong, powerful and even heroic. This strength is shown in Heaney's simple but powerful language. For Larkin, childhood was simply 'nothing' and he is more concerned about the conventional adventures of fictional characters that did not happen to him. This is reflected in his conventional verse form as well as in some of the clichéd images he uses.

KEY TERMS

Make sure you understand these terms before moving on!

■ theme
■ key words
■ PEC

Writing on poetic technique

Essays in an English Literature exam

Poems communicate their ideas in many different ways and you will frequently need to comment on their **form** (the way they are written) as well as their **content** (what they say). Generally speaking content is more important in English exams whilst form is more important in Literature exams.

- Content includes subject, theme and setting
- Form includes **poetic techniques** such as imagery, simile, metaphor, alliteration, etc. and metrical forms such as the use of ballads, dramatic monologues or sonnets.

Content comparisons are discussed in the section on *Comparing cultural texts* (p 72). A 'content' comparison can also be based on readers' reactions, as in a question that asks you to discuss 'poems that some people might find disturbing'.

Remember in literature exams even when poems are grouped by content you should try to include some discussion of form.

Discussing poetic technique

In Literature exams you will often be asked to look at poems from before 1914. These tend to be more formal in their use of poetic techniques like figurative language, specific verse forms and rhyme schemes.

Writing about form 1

When you are choosing a second poem to write about in the exam you need to ask yourself the following questions:

- Does the second poem use imagery in a similar or different way to the first?

- Do the poems make similar or different language choices?

- How have the two poems made use of similar or different poetic forms?

- Are there similarities or differences in rhyme and metre?

This type of response can be very open ended and you need to choose poems that are 'rich' enough in language to provide material for you to discuss.

You could consider the poems' use of:

- Unusual or striking word play

- Similes, metaphors and other figurative language

- Rhyme schemes

- Nature (or death, or time, etc) imagery

- Colloquial language

- Sonnet or ballad forms.

Writing about form 2

For a poetic form (sonnet, dramatic monologue) essay you need to:
- Have a good grasp of the rules of the form – e.g. rhyme scheme, use of persona
- Be able to discuss how each poem uses the form
- Be able to discuss how the poets adapt the form for their own purposes
- Be able to assess how effective the use of the form is.

Balance

You may find some poems easier to discuss than others but it is important to keep your discussion as balanced as possible. Write approximately the same amount on each poem.

Features to look out for in a poem

If your named poem was 'A Song (Lying is an occupation)' you might make the following notes.

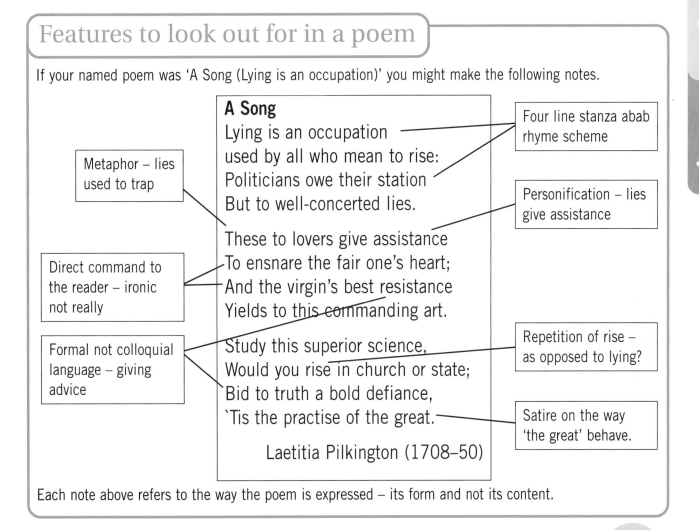

Metaphor – lies used to trap

Direct command to the reader – ironic not really

Formal not colloquial language – giving advice

A Song
Lying is an occupation
used by all who mean to rise:
Politicians owe their station
But to well-concerted lies.

These to lovers give assistance
To ensnare the fair one's heart;
And the virgin's best resistance
Yields to this commanding art.

Study this superior science,
Would you rise in church or state;
Bid to truth a bold defiance,
'Tis the practise of the great.

Laetitia Pilkington (1708–50)

Four line stanza abab rhyme scheme

Personification – lies give assistance

Repetition of rise – as opposed to lying?

Satire on the way 'the great' behave.

Each note above refers to the way the poem is expressed – its form and not its content.

KEY TERMS

Make sure you understand these terms before moving on!
- form
- content
- poetic techniques

Different cultural texts (EN2)

English from around the world

What you may study

You will either study a number of poems, or short stories or novels written by English speakers from different countries around the world. Whether you write about these texts for coursework or for your final exams depends upon the specification of the exam board that your school is following. Whatever you study, you will need to adopt the same approach. In your coursework or exam answers you will need to:

- show that you understand what you have read and know how it **relates** to other texts in 'Different Cultures'
- display an **awareness** of the themes and ideas in the texts which make them **distinctive**
- make comparisons between the texts in your essays. The current AQA Anthology provides two clusters of poems from different cultures. You will need to study only one of these clusters.

Finding links between the poems

Look for common ideas or themes that can help you make links between the stories or poems you study. Among such ideas and themes try to find:

- ideas about language, power and dialect
- feelings about being caught between two cultures
- feelings about change or how things do not change
- ideas about language and identity
- differences in attitudes and values
- beliefs and ritual
- customs and traditions
- protest against ideas and attitudes (this will include racism)
- feelings about independence.

How you will be graded

To achieve grades C to A* or higher you will need to compare the texts. As you do so you should:

- show an understanding of the texts' main characters
- give a sustained and developed knowledge of the texts and show an awareness of the writers' purposes
- show insight and the ability to explore these texts
- reveal a **structured understanding** of how **thoughts** and **feelings** are revealed in the texts
- display an awareness of how form, language and imagery are used and comment on how these contribute towards meaning in the texts
- make effective use of textual detail to support your arguments. At higher levels reveal a convincing and imaginative **interpretation** of the texts
- show involvement through personal **empathy**. That is, appreciate the writer's concerns, ideas or attitudes. At the higher levels you will exhibit a high degree of empathy
- place people and powerful **emotions** in the context of local customs and traditions.
- engage with texts by showing an enthusiastic **personal response**.

Some essential poetic terms

Use of letter and word sounds

- Alliteration: the same consonant at the beginning of words repeated for an effect: 'fireside flickers'.
- Assonance: repetition of vowel sounds for an effect: 'icy winds knife us'. The repetition of the vowel 'i' helps stress the coldness of the 'winds'.
- Onomatopoeia: words which sound like their meaning: 'buzz' and 'click'.
- Rhythm and rhyme: the poem's pace when read aloud and word endings that sound alike for an effect.

Imagery

- Metaphor: a stronger comparison where 'is' or 'are' is used or implied: 'Juliet is the sun.'
- Personification: ('person-making'): giving an animal, idea or noun human feelings to enhance an emotion, feeling or effect: 'Arise fair sun and kill the envious moon.'
- Oxymoron: figures of speech in which contradictory, opposite words are yoked together for an effect. For example, The Beatles, the great 1960s' pop band, famously had a hit song and a film entitled *A Hard Day's Night*.
  Oxymorons can also be paradoxes to enliven prose but some have turned into clichés: 'act naturally', 'living dead', etc.
- Simile: a comparison using 'as' or 'like': 'My love is as deep as the sea.'

Punctuation and form

- Ballad: a story poem that usually features dramatic stories about ordinary people.
- Couplet: a two-line stanza that rhymes.
- Caesura or cesura: means 'a cutting'. It can be any type of punctuation in poetry that causes the reader to pause. Poets use them to end-stop their lines and to emphasise points and ideas in their poetry. A caesura can add a great deal of meaning if placed in the middle of a line.
- Elegy: a poem for a dead person.
- Enjambment or run-on line/run-on stanza: one line runs into another to achieve a poetic effect, often used to aid rhythm and help enact something.

- Free verse: irregular stanzas, filled with lines of varying length. The lines are like waves coming in along a sea-shore: each has natural rhythm and is just long enough. The form suits conversational and argumentative poems. Free verse, or vers libre, was the most popular form of poetry in the twentieth century and still remains so.
- Lyric: a poem that sets out the thoughts and feelings of a single speaker.
- Quatrain: four lines of a poem that rhyme. It is the main unit in English poetry.
- Stanza: one of the divisions of a poem, composed of two or more lines and easily identified by a common pattern of meter, rhyme and number of lines.
- Sonnet: usually a 14-line poem about a serious theme such as love or death.
- Triplet or Tercet: a three-line stanza; this is a form suited for comic poetry, but watch out for when poets reverse the expected content, as with Seamus Heaney's *Mid-Term Break*. The effect can be very poignant.
- Verse: an entire poem or collection of poems or poetry.

Narrative stance and attitudes within poems

- Narrator (first and third person): if the whole poem is spoken by the first-person narrator, who is clearly not the poet, then this is known as a dramatic monologue. For an example, read Robert Browning's poem *My Last Duchess*.
- Tone: a poet's or narrator's attitude towards their subject and audience. Note that tone can change within a poem to emphasise changes of meaning. The poet's use of diction (words deliberately chosen for their associations and sounds) can affect the tone of a poem. For example, contrasts between multi-syllable and one-syllable words can very quickly change the mood of a poem. In Carol Ann Duffy's poem *Education for Leisure*, the contrast between the fizzy polysyllabic 'pavements suddenly glitter' and the monosyllabic 'I touch your arm' is very chilling indeed.

KEY TERMS

- relates
- awareness
- distinctive
- structured understanding
- thoughts
- feelings
- interpretation
- empathy
- emotions
- personal response

QUICK TEST

1. What is a simile?
2. Explain what empathy means.
3. Give an example of onomatopoeia.
4. What is the difference between 'verse' and a 'stanza'?
5. What is a suitable subject for a sonnet and why?

Comparing cultural texts (EN2)

You have to write a comparative essay comparing two or more texts. On these pages there are examples of what you should try to achieve. Your first aim in exams is to write about poems that are naturally linked through themes, ideas, or layout. See the previous pages for suggestions on linking the poems or texts.

- Write about the importance of language and form in *Half-Caste* (by John Agard) and *Unrelated Incidents* (by Tom Leonard).

What the poems are about

1. Both poems deal with issues of language, power and prejudice.
2. Leonard ironically reverses the usual dialects associated with authority and reading the news (received pronunciation and standard English). He wants us to think about issues of truth and authority when we only hear the news read by people with received pronunciation or standard English.
3. He argues that it is wrong and prejudiced to believe that these dialects are the only ones capable of expressing the truth and so be taken seriously. His angry narrator shows that such prejudice is silly and wrong, especially as the narrator argues that his working-class Glaswegian dialect is the only one which should be taken seriously; it is as if the local dialect is a cut above anyone else's because it is the only one capable of expressing the 'trooth'. Leonard infers that 'trooth' can be told in any dialect.
4. The tone of his poem is one of anger against the prejudices of society where working-class dialects are not taken seriously and given no respect. Leonard thinks that speakers of local dialects are not given the consideration and status that they deserve.
5. Agard's narrator eloquently shows, through a number of unusual and convincing comparisons, that it is wrong to label anyone by using the term 'half-caste'. The unquestioned use of such terms can lead to the prejudice of seeing someone as only half a person.
6. Agard and Leonard show us that power, authority and prejudice are linked with language and how we use it. They warn us against blindly accepting some dialects, such as standard English, as voices of authority and correctness while excluding others and their speakers as only worthy of ridicule. The 'truth' can be expressed in other dialects too.

How meaning in the poems is expressed

- The impact of each poem's argument is enhanced through being spoken by a first-person narrator. Both are appropriately set out in free verse, in which the dialect is defiantly proclaimed and phonetically spelt in lines of varying length. The narrowness of the poems' lines contrast with other poems written in standard English. The poets may intend the form of their poems to act as a badge for the dignity, independence and truthfulness of their dialects. The form of each poem is thus appropriate for the arguments and language deployed by the poets.
- The rules of standard English have no place in these poems as there is no punctuation, nor capital letters. The narrators make their points with questions, arguments and statements. The idea is to advance an alternative to standard English. Agard's poem has stanzas in which some of the senses are alluded to. Leonard's poem is plainer, using a single stanza or verse paragraph to refer to speech and Glaswegian dialect. The poets may be from different parts of the world yet there is a similarity in their views on language about what should be said and how it should be expressed.
- Both poems have an ironic tone intended to startle their audiences into accepting the truth of the arguments that they advance. Phrases such as 'belt up' and 'ah rass' disclose their respective tones.

Try to tie the main comparative points of the poems together briefly and give your views.

Half-Caste

1

Excuse me
standing on one leg
I'm half-caste

5

Explain yuself
what yu mean
when yu say half-caste
yu mean when picasso
mix red an green
is a half-caste canvas
explain yuself
wha yu mean
when yu say half-caste
yu mean when light an shadow
mix in de sky
is a half-caste weather
well in dat case
england weather
nearly always half-caste
in fact some o dem cloud
half-caste till dem overcast
so spiteful dem dont want de sun pass
ah rass
explain yuself
wha yu mean
when yu say half-caste
yu mean tchaikovsky
sit down at dah piano
an mix a black key
wid a white key
is a half-caste symphony

Explain yuself
wha yu mean
Ah listening to yu wid de keen
half of mih ear
Ah lookin at yu wid de keen
half of mih eye
and when I'm introduced to yu

I'm sure you'll understand
why I offer yu half-a-hand
an when I sleep at night
I close half-a-eye
consequently when I dream
I dream half-a-dream
an when moon begin to glow
I half-caste human being
cast half-a-shadow
but yu must come back tomorrow
wid de whole of yu eye
an de whole of yu ear
an de whole of yu mind

6

an I will tell yu
de other half
of my story

John Agard

Unrelated Incidents

2

this is thi
six a clock
news thi
man said n
thi reason
a talk wia
BBC accent
iz coz yi
widny wahnt
mi ti talk
aboot thi
trooth wia
voice lik
wanna yoo
scruff. if
a toktaboot
thi trooth
lik wanna yoo
scruff yi
widny thingk
it wuz troo.
jist wanna yoo
scruff tokn.
thirza right
way ti spell
ana right way
ti tok it. this
is me tokn yir
right way a
spellin. this
is ma trooth.
yooz doant no
thi trooth
yirsellz cawz
yi canny talk
right. this is
the six a clock
nyooz. belt up.

3

4

Tom Leonard

Important Point

In an exam you will be unlikely to write as much as this. You will also need to give more brief quotations to support your points than are given above. Even so, a few points made well with appropriately chosen evidence would secure you a good mark.

INTERNET

Help with exam poetry and texts can be found at:
www.englishresources.co.uk

Practice questions

Use the questions to test your progress. Check your answers on page 95.

How to read and study poetry

1. How many poems do you have to write about in your Literature exam?

   ....

2. Are you being tested on your reading or your writing?

   ....

3. Name two forms for poems.

   ....

4. How many times should you read your poems?

   ....

5. What is tone?

   ....

6. What are the main forms of narration?

   ....

7. Diction is another word for the word choices that poets make for their poems. True or false?

   ....

8. What is a theme?

   ....

9. Part of a poem is a verse. True or false?

   ....

10. Which other post-1914 poet will you study if you are reading Simon Armitage?

    ....

11. The classroom 'glowed like a sweet shop' is a metaphor. True or false?

    ....

12. Name the post-1914 poet that is paired with Gillian Clarke.

    ....

How to write about poems

13. How many poems do you need to compare in your final English exam?

    ....

14. What is enjambment?

    ....

15. What does it mean to 'compare and contrast' when writing about poetry?

    ....

16. What is an oxymoron?

    ....

17. What can an oxymoron suggest?

    ....

18. Quatrains are the main units of English poetry. True or false?

    ....

19. What is free verse?

    ....

20. Why is free verse appropriate for certain poems?

....

21. What is assonance?

....

22. Where should you give your personal view of the poems that you write about?

....

Texts from different cultures

23. What are 'Texts from Different Cultures'?

....

24. What form is most favoured by poets from 'Different Cultures'?

....

25. Identify two dialects spoken by poets from other cultures.

....

26. Name three texts by writers or poets of 'Different Cultures' from the exam syllabus that you are following.

....

27. Give three themes or ideas that can be explored in these texts.

....

28. Once you identify a figure of speech or some other poetic technique what must you do afterwards?

....

29. John Agard uses no caesuras in his poem. True or false?

....

30. The narrow lines of Tom Leonard and John Agard's poems suit the dialect that they use. True or false?

....

31. Why do Tom Leonard and John Agard use free verse?

....

32. In his poem *Half-Caste*, John Agard argues that the unthinking use of the standard English phrase 'half-caste' leads to negative implications. What are these implications?

....

33. How long do you have to plan and write your essay in the final exam?

....

34. Identify two poems from 'Different Cultures' in the AQA Anthology that are connected by the theme of change. If you are studying with another exam board identify a theme that is present in two or more texts.

....

35. How many clusters do you study?

....

How well did you do?   0–9 Try again   10–19 Getting there   20–29 Good work   30–36 Excellent!

Novels and short stories

Texts studied

Novels and short stories are studied as part of the English and English Literature specifications. For the AQA English exam you must study one prose text by an author on the exam board's lists. If you study English and English Literature, the text you study for coursework must be a pre-1914 text, whilst the text you study for the exam must be one of the texts set by the board.

In summary, this means:

English only
- 1 novel or collection of stories – can be pre- or post-1914 – coursework assessed.

English and English Literature
- 1 novel or collection of stories – pre-1914 – coursework assessed in English and in English Literature.
- 1 novel or collection of stories – post-1914 – exam.

To gain the higher grades you will need to demonstrate knowledge of the social, historical or **cultural setting** of the novel or collection of short stories.

Points to remember
- The coursework prose study specifies authors and not titles. You may be able to study a book of your own choice.
- If you choose a collection of short stories, they should be about as demanding as a novel in terms of complexity, range and sustained reading.
- A post-1914 text must be written by an author with a well established critical reputation, and must be worthy of serious study.
- This piece of coursework can be assessed orally.
- Your language and style will affect the impression you create even when they are not being directly assessed.
- Topic sentences introduce points and hold your work together.

How you will be graded

You will be assessed on your ability to read and show your understanding through writing or speaking about your chosen texts.

To achieve C to A* you should aim to:
- show insight into the implications and relevance of a text
- comment on its style, structure and characters
- discuss the writer's use of language.

To get a grade A or better you will need to show analytical and interpretative skills when evaluating:
- the moral, philosophical and social significance of a text
- significant achievements within the prose-fiction genre
- the writer's narrative craft and appeal to the reader
- patterns and details of language exploited for implication or suggestion.

Possible assignment

Assignments that are assessed for both English and English Literature exams are known as 'cross-over' assignments.

These might include the following.

- A **close analysis** of a chapter of a novel. You would need to show its significance to the text as a whole and show awareness of the novel's **historical or social context**. For example, a study of the opening chapter of *Great Expectations* by Charles Dickens.
- An exploration of an author's approach to a character or theme in a novel or range of short stories. You would need to note the effects of social, historical or cultural influences. For example, Charlotte Brontë's exploration of the role of women in *Jane Eyre*.
- An examination of a particular **genre**, such as science fiction or detective stories. You would need to study a range of stories and show a knowledge of literary tradition as well as social, historical or cultural context. For example, a study of the role of the scientist in the stories of H G Wells.
- A comparison of the way an issue or theme, such as relationships between men and women, is treated in a range of short stories, showing awareness of cultural contexts. For example, a study of relationships in the short stories of Thomas Hardy.
- An investigation of an author's use of settings in the novel or group of short stories, showing knowledge of literary contexts. For instance, moor and valley in Emily Brontë's *Wuthering Heights*.
- A structured interview with the teacher about your response to and understanding of key features of a text, the author's choice of language and structure, and the social, historical and cultural context of the text. For instance, a structured interview on Mary Shelley's *Frankenstein*.

If you are entering two coursework prose study assignments, one for English Literature and one for English, you have a wider choice of texts. These might include:

- A study of five or six short stories in the same genre, written by different authors and published before 1914, showing awareness of social, historical and cultural contexts. For instance, a comparative study of stories by Poe and Maupassant (in translation).
- An analysis of technique in a novel by an author not included on the National Curriculum list, such as Bram Stoker's Dracula, showing awareness of literary tradition and social, historical and cultural contexts.

If you are studying English but not English Literature, you could consider:

- a study of William Golding's use of symbolism in *Lord of the Flies*
- an analysis of the importance of one or more characters in a novel
- a study of a writer's technique across a range of short stories.

KEY TERMS

Make sure you understand these terms before moving on!

- cultural setting
- close analysis
- historical context
- social context
- genre

QUICK TEST

❶ How many novels do you have to study if you are taking the English and English Literature option?

❷ How many do you have to study if you are taking the English and English Literature option and wish to write about a novel that is not on the National Curriculum list?

❸ What is the historical context of a novel?

❹ What does 'genre' mean?

❺ It is possible to gain a coursework grade without writing a word. True or False?

Literary technique (EN2)

What to look for in characters

When you are studying the characters in your novel, you should look out for the following things.

- The names of characters sometimes tell you more about them. For example, Pip from *Great Expectations* is named after a seed. One of the novel's main themes is his development and growth as he changes from a lower-class boy to a gentleman. The novel charts the education of his heart as well as his mind.
- What characters look like. The physical appearance of characters given in their description often tells us more about them.
- What a character says and does. Much can be inferred from talk and action.
- Flat and round characters. E.M. Forster created these terms to describe types of characters found in novels in his book *Aspects of the Novel* (1927). Flat characters do not develop in novels and are generally not as important as round characters, who develop because they change in the course of a novel. The same terms can be applied to characters in short stories.
- How a character interacts with other characters.
- What other characters say about him or her. This can help readers understand other aspects of a character's personality.
- Any direct comments on the character by a third-person narrator.
- If the character that you are studying is the narrator of your story, how far can you trust what he or she says? Do they have self-knowledge or do they have a lot to learn? Could they be termed an unreliable narrator?

 Always check to see if a story is written in the first or third person.

First- or third-person narrator?

- Notice how writers tell their stories. Do they tell the story from the point of view of a character within the story as 'I' or 'me' – that is, as a **first-person narrator**? Or have they chosen to write about the story from the point of view of someone who looks at what is going on from outside the story and in which the narrator says 'he', 'she' or 'they'? The writer's choice of who tells the story can determine how we see, understand and interpret characters, as well as themes and ideas within a story.
- First-person narrators usually have a limited point of view. They are so close to what is happening that they cannot see everything that is going on or know what other characters are thinking.
- **Third-person narrators** can see and know much more. They can know everything if the writer wants them to. This last kind of narrator is called an omniscient narrator.
- It is important to understand that whatever the first- or third-person narrator thinks is not necessarily what the writer thinks. Show in your writing that you understand that writers adopt masks by using narrators in their stories.

Dialogue

Dialogue, speech between two or more characters:
- makes characters seem more vivid and lifelike.
- helps readers learn about characters. Their aims, motives, personalities and outlooks are shown in what they say and how they say it.
- shows what characters think about other characters.
- helps readers to make up their minds about characters using 'first hand' evidence.

Third-person narration and **characterisation**: Doris Lessing's *Flight*

'Hey!' he shouted; saw her jump, look back, and abandon the gate. Her eyes veiled themselves, and she said in a pert neutral voice: 'Hullo, Grandad.' Politely she moved towards him, after a lingering backward glance at the road.

'Waiting for Steven, hey?' he said, his fingers curling like claws into his palm.

'Any objection?' she asked lightly, refusing to look at him.

He confronted her, his eyes narrowed, shoulders hunched, tight in a hard knot of pain which included the preening birds, the sunlight, the flowers. He said: 'Think you're old enough to go courting, hey?'

Notice how the author simply tells us what is happening. Some narrators give information on what people are thinking or feeling.

First person narration and dialogue: Sylvia Plath's *Superman and Paula Brown's New Snowsuit.*

The narrator has been wrongfully accused of spoiling Paula Brown's snowsuit.

'I didn't do it.'

But the words came out like hard, dry little seeds, hollow and insincere. I tried again. 'I didn't do it. Jimmy Lane did it.'

'Of course we'll believe you,' Mother said slowly, 'but the whole neighbourhood is talking about it. Mrs Sterling heard the story from Mrs Fein and sent David over to say we should buy Paula a new snowsuit. I can't understand it.'

'I didn't do it,' I repeated, and the blood beat in my ears like a slack drum. I pushed my chair away from the table, not looking at Uncle Frank or Mother sitting there, solemn and sorrowful in the candlelight.

The staircase to the second floor was dark, but I went down to the long hall to my room without turning on the light switch and shut the door. A small unripe moon was shafting squares of greenish light along the floor and the windowpanes were fringed with frost.

Again the author tells us what happened and allows readers to make up their own minds on how she is feeling.

 Remember that it is not enough to identify literary terms in texts. You need to comment on their effectiveness.

Make sure you understand these terms before moving on!

- first-person narrator
- third-person narrator
- dialogue
- characterisation

QUICK TEST

❶ In *Flight* how does the narrator use description of actions to show Grandad's emotions?

❷ What do the granddaughter's short answers show about her attitude.

❸ What does the narrator in *Paula Brown...* say three times?

❹ What does she say about the way she spoke?

❺ What does she say about what she felt. What does this show?

Themes, mood, atmosphere (EN2)

Themes

Themes are ideas or messages that writers explore in their stories. The novel is a form of writing that allows writers to use more than one theme.

- In *Roll of Thunder Hear My Cry* (1976), Mildred D. Taylor explores the theme of growing up and the coming of age of its main character, Cassie Logan. She experiences racism in 1930s' Mississippi, despite her family's best efforts to shield her from its worst aspects. Among other themes, the novel also examines the characters' attachment to the land, family roots, independence and the self-respect that comes from owning parcels of land.

Mood and atmosphere

Writers try to create a mood and atmosphere in stories and novels to illuminate the feelings and actions of their characters. Mood and atmosphere, through the skilful use of description, help set the tone for a piece of writing; this creates a frame of mind for the reader and a sense of expectation of what is to follow. Mood and atmosphere can be achieved by using the following literary effects:

- careful choice of words (diction) which helps suggest an atmosphere and tone
- the length and variety of sentences; short ones can suggest tension
- repetition in sentences of words and phrases
- monologues (speaking to oneself); dreams and day-dreams are good ways of revealing the motives and desires of characters
- similes
- metaphors

- personification
- oxymorons
- alliteration
- assonance
- motifs (words, ideas and imagery which recur in texts)
- the use of the senses: sound, touch, sight, smell and touch
- through the tone of the narrator and his or her closeness to, or distance from, the action.

Choose a passage that moves you from a text that you are reading and try to work out how the writer created the mood and atmosphere of the passage.

Comparing novels and stories

- Both have plots and stories.
- Both may include dialogue.
- Both have characters.
- Both set out themes and ideas.

Short stories differ from novels in that they:
- are usually based upon a specific incident or point in time
- usually have just one main plot and they have

no space for sub-plots or sub-texts
- have less description because there is less space: any description used needs to be economical and essential as it has to add meaning to a story
- use striking details
- sometimes have more fragmented dialogue
- include fewer characters who do and say more in less space than characters in novels.

Comparing short stories

You are more likely to compare short stories than novels in either your exam or coursework. Short stories are usually set in groups and can be by a single **author** or on a particular theme.

Short stories have much less room than novels to develop such things as plot and character. You should therefore look out for some of the following:

Content
What happens in the story?
- Is it a description of a single incident or of a limited time period?
- Is it mostly interested in plot or character?
- What have you learned by the end of the story?

Characterisation
Who is the story about?
Characterisation is important in short stories as they have fewer characters than novels and tend to be more interested in character than plot. In Edgar Allen Poe's story *Murders in the Rue Morge* we are fascinated by the plot details of who committed the murder. In his story *The Tell-Tale Heart,* the interest of the story lies in how the central character copes with being a murderer.
Ask yourself:
- Which characters do I learn about?
- Am I more interested in them than in the incidents described?
- Is the plot simply a way of seeing the character in action?
- How are characters presented? – through dialogue, through the action or via the narrator?

Setting
Where the story takes place.
Setting can be very important in a short story. Some short stories take place in a single room such as Kate Chopin's *The Story of an Hour* or concern themselves entirely with what happens in the heads of their characters. A violent story like Maupassant's *Vendetta* is set in very savage landscape
Questions to ask about setting include:
- How does it affect the plot?
- Does it tell us anything about the characters
- Does it help to create mood?
- How does it relate to the theme?

Narrative technique
Who is telling the story?
The **narrative technique** employed can have a huge impact on our reading of a story. Usually it will be third or first person narration. Consider how the point of view of the story affects our reading of it. Can we always trust first person narrators?

Style
The way in which the story is told.
- What literary features, such as metaphor, simile, personification and symbolism does the author employ?
- What kind of language – formal, colloquial etc is used?
- How does the author vary things like sentence and paragraph length?

Theme
The underlying message of the story. This is likely to be more obvious than in a novel which has room for many themes. For instance in Graham Greene's story *The Destructors*, which is set shortly after the Second World War, a group of boys completely demolish a house. The theme could be vandalism but in fact it is about the effect of adult destruction – the war – on the minds and attitudes of children.
- If the stories you are studying are grouped by theme you will need to consider how each author approaches that theme.
- If you are studying stories by a single author think about what themes occur across the different stories.

Make sure you understand these terms before moving on!

- author
- characterisation
- narrative technique
- setting
- theme

Short stories

Setting and setting up the story

Short stories are often studied for the different cultures section of an exam and the details of a particular place and the attitudes expressed by the characters can often give us a good idea of how people from different cultures view the world.

A good example of this is Maupassant's short story *Vendetta*.

Here is the opening passage.

> Paolo Saverini's widow lived alone with her son in a poor little house on the ramparts of Bonifacio. The town, built on a spur of the mountains, in places actually overhanging the sea, looks across a channel bristling with reefs, to the lower shores of Sardinia. At its foot, on the other side and almost completely surrounding it, is the channel that serves as its harbour, cut in the cliff like a gigantic corridor. Through a long circuit between steep walls, the channel brings to the very foot of the first houses the little Italian or Sardinian fishing-boats, and, every fortnight, the old steamboat that runs to and from Ajaccio.
>
> Upon the white mountain the group of houses form a whiter patch still. They look like the nests of wild birds, perched so upon the rock, dominating that terrible channel through which hardly ever a ship risks a passage. The unresting wind harasses the sea and eats away the bare shore, clad with a sparse covering of grass; it rushes into the ravine and ravages its two sides. The trailing wisps of white foam round the black points of countless rocks that everywhere pierce the waves, look like rags of canvas floating and heaving on the surface of the water.
>
> The widow Saverini's house held for dear life to the very edge of the cliff; its three windows looked out over this wild and desolate scene.
>
> She lived there alone with her son Antoine and their bitch Semillante, a large, thin animal with long, shaggy hair, of the sheep-dog breed. The young man used her for hunting.
>
> One evening, after a quarrel, Antoine Saverini was treacherously slain by a knife-thrust from Nicolas Ravolati, who got away to Sardinia the same night.

If we look carefully at this introduction we will see it does several important jobs.

- The title gives us a clue to what the story will be about (a vendetta is a blood feud carried out when a member of a family is killed).

- The description of the place tells us where in the world we are – it also tells us that this is a very savage and violent place.

- The first sentence tells us about the main character, the widow Savarini.

- By the end of this passage we have met all the main characters in the story.

- We might also be wondering how a helpless widow can possibly be involved in a vendetta.

What we learn about other cultures and traditions

- The description of **place** tells us about conditions in a country other than our own.
- The **behaviour** of the people allows us to compare other lives with ours.
- The **attitudes** expressed by speech and behaviour allow us to compare them with our own.
- We also gain insight in to people's **beliefs** and codes of conduct.

Short stories in the exam

For the short story option you have to compare and contrast one story with another in terms of

- Content
- Characters
- Theme
- Setting
- Style

The two most popular areas for comparison are character and theme, followed by plot. Questions on style and setting are rarer in literature exams but you will often need to pay attention to setting if you are writing about it from the point of view of different cultures and traditions in an English exam.

If you are given a choice make sure that the story you pick is well matched with the named one. You should aim to write about the same amount on each text.

Writing about two short stories is rather like writing about two poems (see pages 64–5). The main difference is that there is a temptation to quote too much of the story as evidence. Keep quotations short and to the point.

Sometimes you will be given the titles of both short stories, sometimes you will be given one title and asked to choose a second one. You need to revise all the stories equally as you don't know which one will be named.

KEY TERMS

Make sure you understand these terms before moving on!

- place
- behaviour
- attitudes
- beliefs

Practice questions

Use the questions to test your progress. Check your answers on page 95.

Novels and short stories

1. What type assessment is used for novels in the English syllabus?
    ....

2. What is the cut-off date for older novels?
    ....

3. If you are studying an older novel, what do you have to check about the author?
    ....

4. What is the historical context of a text?
    ....

5. Are you assessed on reading or writing?
    ....

6. What does 'plot' mean?
    ....

7. What does it mean to 'contrast'?
    ....

8. Explain the term 'genre'.
    ....

9. What is meant by a 'writer's craft'?
    ....

10. Explain what irony means.
    ....

11. What are 'transitions'?
    ....

12. Give two types of themes that you may write about in your assignments.
    ....

Literary technique (EN2)

13. What are the main styles of narration?
    ....

14. From which viewpoint does a first-person narrator tell a story?
    ....

15. Does the author believe what a narrator believes?
    ....

16. What type of narrator can see most in a story?
    ....

17. Give three ways of understanding a character.
    ....

18. What is an 'omniscient narrator'?
    ....

19. What is meant by the terms 'flat' and 'round' characters?
    ....

20. Define what dialogue means.
....

21. Why do writers use dialogue?
....

22. Briefly explain the rules for how dialogue should be set out on the page.
....

23. What is a monologue?
....

24. How can dialogue help you learn more about characters?
....

Themes, mood, atmosphere (EN2)

25. Identify three similarities in novels and short stories.
....

26. Point out three differences between short stories and novels.
....

27. Why do short stories concentrate on mainly one plot?
....

28. Point out three ways in which writers create mood and atmosphere in their stories.
....

29. What is 'diction'?
....

30. Mood and atmosphere sets up a frame of mind and an expectation of what is to follow in a text. True or false?
....

31. Mood and atmosphere can be achieved through the skilful use of description or imagery. True or false?
....

32. Imagery is used only for poetry and not in novels or short stories. True or false?
....

33. Explain the difference between alliteration and assonance.
....

34. What is a theme?
....

35. Give one example of a theme that can be linked with the historical context of a novel or a story.
....

36. Briefly sum up the difference between a short story and a novel.
....

How well did you do? ✗ 0–9 Try again 10–18 Getting there 19–27 Good work 28–36 Excellent! ✓

Exam technique

Planning and reading in exams

- Bring a watch, and two spare pens, etc. so you can manage your time and relieve stress.
- Channel all your nervous energy and adrenaline into your exam and you will be surprised at what you can achieve.
- Question the question! Read the questions very carefully and underline key words and phrases.
- For unseen texts read through written extracts twice: firstly to get the gist of the meaning and then for deeper understanding. Note the development of arguments and ideas as well as how they are expressed by underlining words or by making short, phrase-like notes.
- Brainstorm a brief five point or so plan and then renumber your points in the order in that you will need to write them.

When writing exam answers

- Don't waste time with long introductions – get straight into your answer and remember to use standard English. That is, ensure your writing is formal and avoid abbreviations, unless you are asked to use dialect.
- Show your understanding of texts by reading between the lines and by putting information in your own words. Try to integrate quotations within your writing. Constantly refer back to key words and phrases from questions to ensure relevance.
- Add points to your essay plan while writing in case you forget them.
- Be ruthless and divide your time sensibly according to the marks at stake for each question. Do not get bogged down looking for an extra one or two marks when there is a fresh question with several marks at stake. Spread your effort evenly and aim for an overall mark in your answers. A paragraph or so is fine for six marks but you will need several paragraphs for a 26-mark question. Again, be careful not spend too long on questions with only a few marks at stake.
- Managing time is crucial in exams. Allow yourself five to ten minutes to check your work for errors of sense, spelling and punctuation.

Writing exam questions: key words and phrases

1. **Explain** means to show knowledge and understanding by giving a detailed account of something.
2. **Describe** means to set forth the characteristics or details of something.
3. **Argue** is to maintain a standpoint through logic as you would in an essay.
4. **Inform** means to show knowledge and understanding of something by giving a clear account of it to someone else.
5. **Advise** is similar to inform. It means to help someone come to a decision by giving a balanced account of a range of opinions.

Reading questions for set texts

Practice questions for poetry from different cultures

1. Compare two poems that are linked by a similar theme.

2. Compare the presentation of two cultures and the ways that they are important in *Presents from my Aunts in Pakistan* and one other poem.

3. Compare how the poets present the theme of change in two poems.

Practice questions for the poetry sections of the Anthologies

(Try questions that are appropriate for your Anthology)

1. Compare the ways poets reveal their feelings in two poems.

2. Compare the ways in which the attitudes of the speakers are presented in two or more poems, linking pre-1914 to the post-1914 poems.

3. Compare how the poets present nature in two poems.

   In your chosen poems remember to compare:

   - how the writers use nature

   - how the writers use form, structure and language to present nature.

Practice questions for drama

(Try a question if it is relevant for your exam board.)

1. Is Eliza Doolittle in *Pygmalion* any better off at the end of the play than she was at the beginning? You should consider the historical and social setting of the play in your answer.

2. Which of the characters do you think has learned least from his or her experiences in *An Inspector Calls*?

3. How does Willy Russell make the audience aware of Rita's reasons for doing an Open University course in *Educating Rita*?

4. Choose two moments which are likely to make an audience laugh from *The Caretaker*. Explore these moments showing how they produce comic effects.

5. How does Shakespeare present the characters of Romeo and Juliet when they meet in Act 1, Scene 5 of *Romeo and Juliet*?

Resist the temptation to cram and get a good night's sleep before your exam.

KEY TERMS

Make sure you understand these terms before moving on!

- explain
- inform
- describe
- advise
- argue

The reading sections

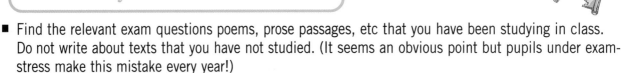

1. When you take the exams

- Find the relevant exam questions poems, prose passages, etc that you have been studying in class. Do not write about texts that you have not studied. (It seems an obvious point but pupils under exam-stress make this mistake every year!)
- Remember that time will be limited. Stick to the advised time limits rigidly as this will help you to build your mark tally over the whole exam. This is successful exam technique!
- Read over the relevant exam sections and questions carefully for the common themes (messages and ideas) in novels, stories, poems or the prose-extracts that you studied. Do not be thrown by unusual wording. Try to establish the underlying themes and ideas that the questions are driving at.

2. How to answer exam questions on media and non-fiction texts

Once you establish the writing's form and purpose you will then be able to produce a more informed answer in which you later show how a writer either informs or persuades their audience.

There are three main questions to ask of any text:
1. What kind of writing is this? Is the writing meant to: entertain, inform, persuade, etc.
2. What is the form of the writing? Is it: an article, leaflet, letter, biography, etc. Does the writer use the first or third person? The second person form of 'You' is known as direct address. Remember that layout and images are an important way of getting messages across. Be prepared to comment on the texts' effectiveness, especially when you are asked to compare one text with another. For instance, how well do the exam texts meet their various purposes?
3. What does the text mean to you? (Audience) What are your motives for reading this text? Do you share its values? How will you interpret it? What does it make you think?

In short:
1. What is the writer trying to say?
2. What means does he or she employ towards effective communication?
3. How successful is the writer in achieving their aims and reaching a given audience?

Reading exam questions: key words and phrases

- 'Use of language' means: word choices, emotive words and phrases to affect the audience, description, persuasive phrases, imagery, alliteration, etc. Avoid saying that the language used 'is very good' which means you do not know what to say!
- 'Style of presentation' means how the text is set out. Think about the text's form. For instance, is it a letter or a newspaper article? Think about the use of underlining, bullet points, statistics, graphs, and pictures. Think about how each of these devices expresses meaning and aids understanding.

- The 'attitude to the reader' is the 'tone of voice' adopted by the writer. Decide if it is, polite, ironic, formal, informal, serious, comic, academic, sarcastic, etc. The tone a writer selects is always related to their purpose and audience.
- **'Convey'** means to get across. For example, "How does the writer convey a sense of ..."
- **"Compare and Contrast"** means "what is similar" and "what is different".
- **Present** means to show or reveal.

How to answer reading questions in the exams

- Write about links between the poems or stories and show your awareness of the main similarities and differences.
- If you are doing the Foundation Exam use the bullet points that are provided for you under your question. You may not be able to answer all the bullet points in the time allowed. You should then aim to do three out of four bullet points and do them as well as you can. Examiners are looking for understanding, knowledge and relevance. *However, be careful not to lose sight of the question and not get lost in answering bullet points!*
- The advice is the same to anyone doing the Higher Paper. Only you sometimes have to brainstorm your own four or five point plan from the question. You should number the points in your plan afterwards to help you produce a structured and fluent answer. Be relevant and focus your answer on key words and phrases from your question.
- **Facts** are things you can prove. For example, Chelsea won the Premier League in 2005 and will do so again in 2006.
- **Opinions** cannot be proved because they are subjective. For instance, 'Chelsea FC will win the Premier League next year!
- Be wary of facts dressed up as opinions. For example, 'Chelsea prefer buying foreign players because they have so many of them in their team.'

 Resist the temptation to cram and get a good night's sleep before your exam.

Tips on persuasive techniques

A knowledge of **persuasive techniques** is particularly useful for this exam.
- Fonts and type-sizes: these are often carefully selected to give points more impact or carry other associations that advertisers would like you to think.
- **Emotive language**: words and phrases that can make you feel strongly about someone or something.
- Humour: when this is used in a controlled way to undermine an opposing point of view it can be very effective.
- Personal testimony: brief quotations from experts or witnesses can be used to verify arguments and make them appear more valid.
- Repetition: this is a form of rhetoric in which you repeat key phrases in your arguments. For example, Firstly, secondly, and thirdly … Dr. Martin Luther King famously repeated the phrase "I have a dream" to great effect in his speech for equality outside the White House in 1968.
- Rhetorical questions: involve an audience and make them think about an issue.
- Underlining, bullet points, statistics, the use of colour, capital letters, bold print, graphics and well chosen pictures with captions can also play an important part in persuading an audience and make information easier to grasp. Remember that colour can connote several meanings and this is usually an important factor in the planning of adverts, leaflets, etc.

KEY TERMS

Make sure you understand these terms before moving on!
- convey
- compare and contrast
- present
- emotive language
- fact and opinion
- persuasive techniques

QUICK TEST

1. How do you recognise the second person (direct address)?
2. What is a fact?
3. Is this a fact or an opinion: "Animal experimentation is wrong."?
4. What is emotive language?

Comprehension: paper 1

English Practice Paper 1 (Higher Tier)
Time allowed: 1 hour and 45 minutes

Information
- The maximum mark for this paper is 54 and the mark allocations are shown in brackets
- Answer in continuous prose

Advice
- Spend about one hour on Section A and about 45 minutes on Section B.

Read Item 1, the extract from The Meat Video Magazine by the British Meat Education Service, Meat and Livestock Commission. This was published as part of edition 9 of a Video Magazine For Secondary Schools – Food Technology and Home Economics.

BEEFY GIRLS
THE VITAL ROLE OF IRON IN THE DIET OF TEENAGE GIRLS

Teenage females are a group which particularly benefits from eating beef, as it is a good source of iron. Iron helps the body in many important processes. For example, it is a vital mineral for blood formation, transport of oxygen, maintenance of the immune system and production of energy. Body tissues and cells depend on oxygen to function properly; if they receive less oxygen, they won't work so well. If iron levels are low, the amount of haemoglobin in our red blood cells, as well as the number of red blood cells, is reduced. This is called anaemia.

Teenage females have the highest rates of iron deficiency anaemia, thought to be due to growth spurts and loss of blood through menstruation. 96% of girls between the age of 11-14 consume less than the recommended intake of iron; the figure is 93% for 15-18 year olds (National Diet and Nutrition Survey 2000).

Teenage females need to consume about 15mg of iron a day and males 11mg.

On average, adult men need 8.7mg of iron a day. For women the figure is 14.8mg.

Food	Serving size	Iron supplied
2 thick slices of lean roast beef	90g	2.3mg

(Food Standards Agency)

TWO TYPES OF IRON
There are two types of iron found in the diet - haem and non-haem iron. Haem iron is found in red meats, bacon, ham and meat products, offal, poultry and game and oily fish. Non-haem iron is found in bread, fortified breakfast cereals, dried fruits, dark green vegetables, peas, beans, lentils, cocoa and eggs.

Haem iron is much more easily absorbed by the body than non-haem iron. Vitamin C helps us to absorb iron, for example drinking fruit juice with a meal, or having vegetables such as broccoli, Brussels sprouts, green peppers or potatoes (all good sources of vitamin C) will help increase our uptake of iron.

If you enjoy eating beef you don't need to eat a lot to benefit from its nutritional value and it won't necessarily cause weight gain. Your students, especially the girls, may be interested to find out more about beef, fat and iron in the diet by visiting the new student mini website on BMES Online www.bmesonline.org.uk.

www.bmesonline.org.uk

Item 2

'You are what you eat' is from a leaflet on 'Nutrition' by *Viva!* and it is subtitled 'Reasons to go veggie'.

you are what you eat

The food we eat is extremely important – so important that it can cause diseases or give protection against them, it can kill you or provide a long and healthy life. Eat nothing but meat and you will die – and fairly quickly. Eat a variety of plant foods – fruits, vegetables, grains, nuts and seeds – and you'll blossom. It's why vegetarians and vegans are less at risk of all the big killer diseases such as heart disease, some cancers, strokes, obesity, diabetes and the other 'degenerative' diseases that mostly afflict the wealthy countries – the countries which eat the most animal products.

Vegetarians

Vegetarians don't eat anything that comes from a dead animal:

• meat (eg beef, pork, bacon and lamb)
• poultry (eg chicken, turkey, ducks, geese and quail)
• fish (also shrimps, prawns, mussels, oysters, scampi, crab and lobster)
• slaughterhouse by products (eg gelatine, animal rennet, lard and other animal fats)

Vegans don't eat anything that comes from an animal, alive or dead – so they avoid milk and other dairy products, eggs and honey as well as the above.

Eat right, live longer

The range of foods that a vegetarian can eat is enormous, so there's nothing difficult about it and no real danger. There are hundreds of cookery books available containing thousands of recipes to spark your imagination and tickle your taste buds. And the sooner you start, the sooner your health is likely to improve because you will be giving up those things that damage your body and eating more of those things that protect it.

All meat contains cholesterol, saturated fat and animal protein – the three things identified by the World Health Organisation as damaging to health. Your body does need fats but good fats, not damaging animal fats.

Meat and animal products are also the main source of food poisoning bugs, which are growing more and more deadly as they become resistant to life-saving antibiotics – a direct result of over-prescribing drugs by doctors and their daily use on factory farms.

DAMAGE LIMITATION

Free radicals
These dangerous substances are created simply by eating, breathing or digesting food. They damage body cells and cause disease. Vast numbers are created when meat is cooked.

Antioxidants
These are the natural remedy for free radicals and mop them up. They are found mostly in fruit, vegetables and other plant foods and protect against disease. There is almost none in meat.

Veggie diets – the truth

An awful lot of nonsense is talked about the dangers of vegetarian diets – lack of protein, iron and calcium being the usual candidates.

• Protein deficiency in western vegetarians is virtually unheard of.
• Vegetarians are no more at risk of iron deficiency than meat eaters.
• Many plant foods contain calcium, very little is lost in the urine.

But it is important to eat sensibly and not swap one bad diet for another. So where do you obtain all the right nutrients your body needs?

(All the world's major health organisations agree.)

EAT YOUR GREENS – and reds and yellows

Green leafy vegetables are amongst the most important of foods. But red and yellow foods, such as peppers and tomatoes, are also important because of the antioxidants they contain. Don't become obsessive but if you can manage to eat something from each of the following groups every day, you can't go wrong.

Cereals – wheat (in wholemeal bread, spaghetti and other pastas), rice (preferably brown), porridge oats, breakfast cereals which contain vitamin B12

Pulses, nuts and seeds – beans (all kinds), peas and lentils, seeds and nuts (all kinds)

Fresh fruit – apples, oranges, pears, plums, bananas, kiwis, mango, grapes, cherries, melon

Fresh vegetables – green leafy ones plus orange or red ones such as carrots, peppers and tomatoes

Soya products – tofu, soya margarine, soya milk, soya mince, veggieburgers and sausages

Oils and fats – vegetable margarines (avoid those containing hydrogenated fats), sunflower, rapeseed, flax and olive oils

Here are just some examples of rich sources of nutrients

PROTEIN
Pulses – peas, baked beans, chick peas, kidney beans, butter beans, lentils
Soya products – vegetarian burgers, sausages, cutlets, mince and nuggets
Grains – porridge oats, wholemeal bread, brown rice, pasta
Nuts and seeds – hazelnuts, almonds, brazil nuts, cashews, peanuts, sunflower seeds, pumpkin seeds

CALCIUM
Broccoli
Leafy green vegetables
Wholemeal bread
Potatoes
Almonds and brazil nuts
Soya milk (fortified)
Soya cheeses
Soya yoghurt

> Daily milk, cheese and yoghurt contain calcium and vitamin B12 but also saturated fat, cholesterol and animal protein, which can be damaging. Free range eggs contain vitamins B12 and D, calcium and omega 3 fats but are rich in cholesterol and animal protein, which can cause disease.

IRON
Pulses – baked beans, other beans, peas and lentils
Leafy green vegetables
Dried fruit – apricots, prunes, dates
Cocoa – chocolate
Seeds – esp. pumpkin

GOOD FATS
Essential fats, such as omega 3, are mostly found in plant foods. They do exist in oily fish but fish oils contain low levels of poisons – mercury, PCBs, dioxin. Omega 3 from plants gives more protection against heart disease. Olive oil is a monounsaturated fat and is great for cooking – it's thought to reduce cholesterol.
Seeds – linseed (flax), soya, rape, mustard and hemp – and their oils
Pulses – most beans and lentils, including soya beans and the products made from them, such as tofu (bean curd)
Vegetables – cabbage, broccoli, spinach, kale and avocados

Comprehension: paper 1

Section A: Reading

Answer all questions in this section
You are advised to spend about one hour on this section

1 Read Item 1, the extract called 'Beefy Girls' from the British
Meat Service's Video Magazine For Secondary Schools –
Food Technology and Home Economics.
(a) What are the main arguments in favour of teenage (6 marks)
females eating beef?
(b) Explain how the uses of facts and opinions might encourage (4 marks)
teenagers to eat beef.

Read Item 2 'You are what you eat' by *Viva!* It is from their second in a series of leaflets called
'Reasons To Go Veggie Part 2' about how young people can become vegetarian.
(c) Compare the views about nutrition in Item 1 with the views (6 marks)
about nutrition in Item 2.

2 Look again at Item 2, 'You are what you eat'
(a) How is language used to persuade young people to go vegetarian? (4 marks)
(b) How does the form and presentation of either Item 1 (7 marks)
or 2 help support its claims and arguments?

Section B: Writing to argue, persuade or advise

Answer one question from this section
You are advised to spend 45 minutes on this section

Either

3 Write the text for a leaflet which argues in favour of eating beef. (27 marks)

Or

4 Write the text for a speech that argues the case for a (27 marks)
healthy menu from the school or college's canteen.

Or

5 Write an article for a teenage or school magazine in which (27 marks)
you give specific advice on nutrition.

Or

6 Write a speech in which you aim to persuade younger pupils/students (27 marks)
about the benefits of eating healthily.

Punctuation and oral work

Quick test answers

Page 7 Punctuation again!
1. So that you can be clearly understood.
2. You should use them: for titles of books, to introduce speech, in acronyms, as initials, in letters, as adjectives for proper nouns, to begin sentences and in days, months, names and holidays.
3. a) 'What's the capital of Portugal, Anthony?' b) My favourite Christmas song of all time is "Fairytale of New York" by The Pogues and Kirsty MacColl.
4. Monday, Atlantic, Westlife, RSPCA, Christmas and Louise.

Page 9 End of sentence punctuation
1. Semi-colons.
2. They link two closely related phrases or separate sets of items in a list where there are commas within the sets.
3. It usually expresses a single idea.
4. Yes.
5. Yes.
6. It links another phrase which expands upon the meaning of the first, or punctuates dialogue in plays.

Page 11 Uses for commas
1. They can mark off a list and phrases within a sentence. They are also used within direct speech.
2. Good Heavens!
3. No.
4. Phil said, 'Buy the latest team shirt.'/'It is too expensive,' said Paul.
5. Either title marks, underlining or italics.

Page 13 Apostrophes
1. False
2. False
3. True
4. True
5. False
6. True

Page 15 Sentences
1. False
2. True
3. False
4. False: it is a command or an instruction.
5. True

Page 17 Spellings
1. An examiner is the person doing the examining; an examinee is the person being examined.
2. Donor, donee; nominator, nominee; payer, payee; trainer, trainee. The other half of the pair for words like refugee and evacuee is not used.
3. The 'l' is doubled in fulfilling to keep the 'i' sound short.

Page 21 Linking words and phrases
1. Paragraphs help readers follow your ideas. They also break up too much text which readers can find off-putting.
2. in the same way, similarly, equally, as with, likewise, compared with, an equivalent (any of these).

3. To 'compare' is to look for similarities and to 'contrast' is to look for differences.
4. indeed, in particular, above all, notably, specifically, more importantly, especially, significant(ly), in fact (any of these)
5. They help you make extra points or ideas.

Page 23 Improving writing style
1. a) because b) pink c) now.
2. The readers could lose sight of your meaning.
3. For instance, 'Shoot yourself in the foot'. The image has little impact because it is overused.

Page 25 Speaking and listening
1. Three: a single, drama focus and group.
2. Formal English: use it in formal situations.
3. It helps people understand you and makes your speech more interesting.
4. With family and friends.
5. Conversations need listeners too. You can make better points.

Page 27 Preparing and giving a talk
1. It helps you give a better structure and give detail.
2. Ask questions or show them props, etc.
3. Not reading your speech as this prevents you from getting marks.

Page 28–29 Practice questions

Punctuation and sentences
1. You need to punctuate your work so that your readers will fully understand your meaning.
2. Check your answer against page 7. (Award yourself a mark if you got all five.)
3. Jemma, Great Expectations, English, the first She, Charles Dickens and Easter.
4. Full stop, semi-colon, colon, exclamation mark and question mark.
5. They join closely related sentences; they separate sets of items in lists when there are commas within the sets or lists.
6. A question to which you do not expect a direct answer. You expect instead that your listener will agree with you.
7. Colons can introduce a list; they can introduce a sentence which expands upon the meaning of the first sentence; they can also introduce long quotations that are separated from the writer's prose.
8. Inverted commas are needed for words spoken; the speech needs to be separated from the rest of the writing by a punctuation mark; it is introduced with a capital letter; you need a new line for each speaker; and each new line should be indented three spaces from the margin.
9. Apostrophes can indicate possession or an abbreviated word or phrase.
10. Before the 's' as with the firemen's equipment.
11. Statements, exclamations,

instructions or commands and questions.
12. The main clause is 'I will go to the cinema'. The dependent clause is 'as soon as I have done the washing up'.

Spelling and expression
13. Spelling phonetically sounding out each syllable:
Look–Cover–Say
Write–Check
Use a dictionary; produce a mnemonic.
14. It is 'i' before 'e' except after 'c'.
15. There is a consonant before the 'y' as with 'city'; so it's 'cities'.
16. There is a vowel before the 'y' as with 'monkey'; so it's 'monkeys'.
17. They are all to do with place.
18. Beginning, appearance, interested, grammar, tongue, definitely, necessity, rhythm, sentence.
19. Synonyms are words that mean the same.
20. Homophones are words that are different yet sound the same. For instance, 'whether' and 'weather'.
21. Connective words link phrases, sentences and paragraphs together.
22. To help signpost ideas and arguments so that readers can follow what you mean.
23. Paragraphs break up forbidding chunks of text and make meaning clear. Writers need them to organise their main points and ideas.
24. The topic sentence is the main sentence in a paragraph. The remaining sentences expand on its meaning.
25. 'Control' is the ability to write sentences and paragraphs of appropriate length with control over expression. Word choices and punctuation will also be appropriate and accurate.
26. Because.

Speaking and listening
27. Three.
28. Single, paired and group orals.
29. Local speech particular to an area. It is informal speech.
30. Cockney, Geordie, Scouse, Brummie. There are many others!
31. Formal English used by teachers, doctors, lawyers, in business, etc.
32. Use local dialect with your friends and family. This is because it is friendly and informal; use standard English in formal situations to people with whom you are doing business and do not know.
33. You should note details such as the type of oral and the topic; you will need the date, some notes on your preparation; you should record how the oral went by making a self-assessment so you can set targets for your next oral.
34. Non-verbal language such as eye contact, hand gestures, etc.
35. Register is the tone you adopt when addressing various audiences; for example you

should speak to a judge more formally than you would to a friend.
36. We are being ironic if the tone of our voices implies the opposite meaning of words we use.
37. Good listeners have better, more complex conversations. They have good turn-taking skills too.
38. To 'work out', to 'unpick', to 'unravel'.
39. Debates, topical issues in the news; or an issue that came out of a class text.
40. You are assessed on your ability to talk, not to read. Long, written passages prevent fluency in speech because of the temptation to look at them for reassurance.
41. The 'structure' of your talk is the clarity and order of its presentation.
42. Self-assessment is crucial for setting new targets for improvement and achieving them.

Writing and the media

Quick test answers

Page 33 Story planning and writing
1. By a character in the story, using 'I'.
2. A kind of writing, for example, detective stories, romance, science-fiction, etc.
3. An interesting 'hook' which will seize the attention of an audience.
4. It means going into detail or extensive description.
5. Build up a profile for them; try to give them realistic speech.

Page 35 Non-fiction writing
1. Leaflet or an article on an issue.
2. Rambling or digressive – passing from one subject to another.
3. Proof-reading.
4. At least two.
5. Libraries, encyclopedias, the Internet, knowledgeable people, associated organisations.

Page 37 How to write essays
1. Understanding the whole question and paying attention to key words and phrases.
2. Any book, play or poem in any genre.
3. The period in which the text was written and what was going on at the time.
4. Three or four.
5. At the end and nowhere else.

Pages 44–45 Practice questions

Original writing
1. Writing.
2. Around 1000 words.
3. Story line.
4. Kind of writing. For example, detective or horror stories.
5. They use 'as' or 'like' in the comparison.
6. An interesting beginning which draws the reader in.
7. The setting is where the story is supposed to be in time and place.
8. Check your answer with 'What

You Can Write About' on page 31.
9. Writing that you have created yourself.
10. First and third person.
11. Third person.
12. The plan or outline of the story.
13. Notes, brainstorm or spidergram.
14. Fluency of expression and punctuation.
15. Linear is a 'straight line'. There is no going backwards or forwards as the story unfolds. For example, Romeo and Juliet is a linear play because the action takes place over four days.

Writing: non-fiction

16. Not made up.
17. Check your answer with 'What You Can Write About' on page 34. Any similar matches will be fine.
18. It means 'to ramble'. You could write about anything.
19. You can get information from knowledgeable people, libraries, the Internet, encyclopedias, companies, embassies, etc.
20. No.
21. The intended audience. Some authors target their novels at early readers; others go for the 10- to 14-year-old market.
22. Newspaper and magazine articles, leaflets, advertising posters, letters, petitions, proclamations, essays, reviews, etc. Anything like these would be fine.
23. Any piece of writing.
24. Instructions for: making a meal; finding directions to somewhere; putting a computer together; a booklet on how to keep fit, etc. Anything like this.
25. Yes.
26. To 'compare' is to examine what is similar; to 'contrast' is to say what is different.
27. The 'historical context' includes the events and ideas present at the time when the text was written or set.
28. You need a plan, an introduction, main body and a conclusion. It helps if you have a consistent argument too.
29. At the end of your essay.
30. This is essay technique: you make a 'point', give some appropriate 'evidence' for your point and 'comment', if you can do so.

Media coursework

31. Mood and atmosphere
32. High-key and low-key lighting.
33. Diegetic and non-diegetic sound
34. To aid 'continuity' – that is, to make a smooth transition between scenes.
35. It is a French term that means everything that is 'put on stage' or can be seen in a frame or scene.
36. • TS = Total shot
   • ES = Establishing shot
   • CU = Close up
   • MS = Medium shot
   • POV = Point of view shot
37. C.G.I.
38. The camera tracks forward or back from a character or action, usually on fixed tracks.
39. A straight cut
40. A number of shots/scenes follow in quick succession as in a film trailer.

Shakespeare

Quick test answers

Page 47 Shakespeare assignment
1. Write an essay; you could also, for example, write the stage directions of a director for a scene or two of a play.
2. Brief quotations from the play that are used as evidence for points in essays.
3. It is elevated speech and it invests its speakers with dignity. Nobles, for example, often use it.
4. For moments of high drama and intense feeling.

Page 49 Structure and themes
1. It is the play's main message or idea. There can be several themes in a play.
2. Near the end.
3. The plan or outline of the play.
4. The events and ideas around at the time when the text was written.
5. It would help you understand the whole play and know how speeches could be interpreted. Shakespeare wanted his plays to be heard and seen, not just read.

Page 51 Shakespeare's imagery
1. b 2. d 3. a 4. b 5. c

Page 53 An essay on Caliban
1. From what they say, what they do and from what others say about them you can discover more from any imagery associated with them.
2. Shakespeare mainly wrote history, tragedy and comedy plays.
3. Dramatists wrote soliloquies for important characters to help audiences understand the thoughts, feelings and motives of these characters.

Pages 58–59 Practice questions

Shakespeare assignment
1. Check 'What you may study' on page 46 for possible suggestions. You may study other Shakespeare plays.
2. Read passages for general understanding or the gist first; then read for deeper meaning.
3. Check your answer with 'What you have to do' on page 47. There are other possibilities too.
4. Words and phrases cited from the play (text) as evidence in your writing.
5. Yes.
6. People produce new readings and interpretations of texts according to ideas and values, considered to be important in their time.
7. Imagery and the use of alliteration, assonance, onomatopoeia, etc.
8. History, Tragedy and Comedy. There is a sub-genre: Tragi-comedy.
9. What was then thought about the principles underlying human conduct and nature; how people thought the world worked, beliefs, etc.
10. Poetic verse, blank verse and prose.
11. For the end of scenes and scenes of dramatic intensity.
12. To show dignified speech; speech that helps convey feeling and mood.

Structure and themes
13. A sense of normality and order. 'All is well with the world'.
14. Problems are introduced and order begins to break down.
15. The point of highest dramatic intensity before the protagonist's fall.
16. Battles, unmasking, deaths, marriages etc.
17. Order is restored and the right people are back in control.
18. A central idea or ideas.
19. Check your answers with those in 'Some Themes, Ideas, or Messages which recur throughout the plays' on page 48. There are other themes.
20. Love, appearance and reality, good and evil, identity and disguise, etc.
21. A comic scene is followed by a serious scene.
22. This makes a scene appear even more intense or light-hearted because of the contrasting emotions of the previous scene.
23. Self-knowledge is the ability to see and learn from your faults when others point them out to you. Characters who do so 'develop'.
24. Order – problems – chaos – climax – resolution with new order.

Imagery and essay plans
25. Any kind of imagery or decorative language with alliteration, etc.
26. A comparison using 'as' or 'like'. For instance, 'Clare is like a flower'.
27. It is a comparison which implies or states that something is something else: 'Clare is a flower'.
28. A metaphor that runs or is 'extended' over several lines or a scene.
29. It means 'person-making'. It is powerful metaphor in which things or ideas are given human traits for an enhanced literary effect.
30. Two opposite nouns yoked together for effect: 'A Hard Day's Night'.
31. A character, theme or image that recurs.
32. Imagery helps say more about points made in dialogue and action. It reinforces and enhances the audience's ideas of the characters. It can magnify or draw attention to themes/issues in the text.
33. Characters speak with irony when they say something that is truer than they realise.
34. It is dramatically ironic when the audience knows something important that characters do not. Sometimes this is complicated by one character knowing what another does with the audience sharing their knowledge.
35. Passages and scenes of dramatic intensity. An example is where Romeo first speaks with Juliet.
36. It includes figurative language, including word-pictures like similes and metaphors.

Poetry

Quick test answers

Page 61 Reading set poems
1. 15%.
2. A narrative poem.
3. At the end of your essay.

4. At least three times.
5. Identifying with the theme or idea in a poem or perhaps the narrator's point of view.

Page 63 Writing about poetry (EN2)
1. A 'cut'. The term refers to any punctuation mark used in poetry.
2. 14.
3. Repetition of consonants for an effect, for instance, the headline, 'Football Fever'.
4. A structured bank of phrases designed to help your writing flow.

Page 71 Different cultural texts (EN2)
1. A comparison using 'as' or 'like'.
2. An appreciation of a writer's or narrator's concerns and ideas.
3. Buzz (or any word that sounds like its meaning).
4. 'Verse' is an entire poem or collection of poems; a 'stanza' is a section of a poem.
5. 'Love' or 'death' because sonnets usually have serious subject matter.

Pages 74–75 Practice questions

How to read and study poetry
1. Four.
2. Reading.
3. Free-verse, quatrains, couplets, sonnets etc.
4. At least three.
5. The attitude of the narrator to his or her topic and to the reader.
6. First and third person.
7. True.
8. A key message or idea.
9. False. It is a stanza.
10. Carol Ann Duffy
11. False. It is a simile.
12. Seamus Heaney.

How to write about poems
13. Two or more. Do not write about too many as your comments could be too thinly stretched.
14. A run-on line. Poets use them for effect.
15. To 'compare' is to note what is 'similar'; to 'contrast' is to explain what is different.
16. A figure of speech and a paradox in which two contradictory terms are brought together for an effect: 'awfully nice' and 'alone together'.
17. Usually mixed feelings or a paradox.
18. True. They are composed of two couplets.
19. Stanzas of irregular length and number.
20. It is an ideal form for conversation and argument.
21. Repetition of vowel sounds for an effect.
22. At the end of your essay. Do give your views because examiners are interested in what you think.

Texts from different cultures
23. These are texts written by speakers of English. The poets and writers use either local dialect or standard English in their texts and they mostly come from parts of the world where Britain once had a colonial influence.
24. Free-verse.
25. Glaswegian and West Indian. Or English dialects from any other part of the world.
26. Check what you have studied with the syllabus of your exam

board. The AQA Anthology concentrates only on poetry with 'Poems from Different Cultures'. Several of the other exam boards include short stories as well as poems.

27. Check your answers against the information on page 70.
28. Comment on it.
29. True.
30. True.
31. Free verse is the most natural form for conversation and argument.
32. John Agard thinks that the unthinking use of the terms and phrases such as `half-caste' can lead to a racist viewpoint of seeing people of mixed race as only half human and unworthy of being treated as equals.
33. Half an hour.
34. Most of them. If you are with another exam board, do any of the themes mentioned in 'Finding Links between the Poems' on page 70 apply to your texts? Try to make a couple of connections and give yourself a mark.
35. One.

Novels and short stories

Quick test answers

Page 77 Novels and short stories
1. Two. One set text and one for coursework.
2. Three. One set text and two for coursework.
3. How it is affected by the time in which it was written.
4. 'Type' – as in romance, Western or detective fiction.
5. True. You can be assessed orally.

Page 79 Literary technique (EN2)
1. 'fingers curling like claws' and 'shoulders hunched, tight in a hard knot of pain' show that he is angry.
2. They show that she is being careful not to upset her grandfather.
3. 'I didn't do it.'
4. She says she sounded insincere.
5. The blood pounding in her ears shows that she was probably blushing.

Pages 84–85 Practice questions

Novels and short stories
1. Coursework.
2. 1914.
3. If he or she is on the National Curriculum list.
4. The time and events which took place when it was written.
5. Reading. However, you will need good writing skills to show your understanding.
6. The outline or structure of a piece of writing.
7. To explain what is different.
8. This refers to the kind or type of writing. For example, romance, adventure, detective, horror, etc.
9. How the writer creates effects through emotive or figurative writing.
10. Saying one thing while meaning another. Also speaking the truth without knowing it.
11. Connectives which allow you to move from one argument or point to another in a fluent manner. They are often key words or phrases that are needed at the beginning of paragraphs

such as 'similarly' or 'on the other hand'.
12. Anything from 'Possible Assignments' on page 77 would do for this answer. Anything sensible will be good enough for a mark.

Literary technique (EN2)
13. First and third person.
14. He or she uses 'I' because they are in the story.
15. Not necessarily. Do not confuse author with narrator.
16. Usually the third person. You can have a third-person omniscient all-seeing narrator.
17. Any of the ways set out on 'What to Look for in Characters' on page 78 will do for this answer.
18. An all-knowing author, usually in third-person stories.
19. Round characters develop because they change in the course of the novel. Flat characters do not change, thus they do not develop.
20. 'Conversation'. Two people speaking.
21. Dialogue makes characters vivid and lifelike. What characters say reveal their motives and personality traits; readers can learn about characters from what other characters say about them.
22. New speaker, new line and indent; begin with a capital letter; introduce with a punctuation mark and use inverted commas.
23. A character speaking alone.
24. The answer is similar to question 21. Look at the last two points of the answer to question 21.

Themes, mood, atmosphere
25. Both have: plots, stories, dialogue, characters, themes and ideas.
26. Stories are shorter and tend to concentrate on an incident and have a shorter time-span for the action; there are also fewer characters with less detail; short stories tend to have one plot and fewer themes. Their dialogue is more fragmented. Description in short stories is more economical.
27. There is not enough space to do otherwise.
28. Through description; the use of imagery; through variety in language and sentences and through the tone of the narrator and his or her closeness to the action.
29. The choice of words chosen by the author.
30. True.
31. True.
32. False.
33. Alliteration is the repetition of initial consonants in words for an effect; assonance is the repetition of similar vowel sounds in words for an effect.
34. The main idea or message of a story.
35. Any sensible idea will be good enough here. Look again at 'Themes' on page 80 to see an example with Roll of Thunder Hear My Cry.
36. Check your answer by referring to Q.26. If you've mentioned a few of them give yourself the mark.

Exam advice

Quick test answers

Page 89 The reading sections
1. The writer uses "you".
2. Something that you can prove.
3. An opinion. It can be argued both ways with facts too!
4. Words and phrases which are meant to make you feel strongly about something.

Pages 90–92 Comprehension: paper 1

Section A: Reading
1. (a) Each of the following would gain a mark: beef is a 'good source of iron'; it's a 'vital mineral for blood formation, transport or oxygen'; eating beef helps 'the immune system', it also helps with 'the production of energy'; it's good for our body tissues and cells; eating beef helps prevents iron deficiency and anaemia.
   (b) 'Teenage girls' benefit most because they have the 'highest rates of iron deficiency anaemia'; 'teenage females need to consume about 15mg of iron a day and males about 11mg.' 'You don't need to eat a lot of beef to gain its nutritional value'. It 'won't necessarily cause weight gain'.
   (c) The British Meat page makes argues that teenage females in particular should eat beef to maintain their daily quota of iron because of the natural risk of blood loss. They also make a case for two types of iron with haem iron mainly received and 'easily absorbed' through eating meat. They downplay the possibility of gaining weight by eating meat.
   The Viva leaflet argues that 'fat', cholesterol' and 'animal protein' in meat is associated with obesity and disease. Viva! stresses the need for 'sensible', 'appropriately planned, vegetarian diets' for a 'long and healthy life'. They make a case against the 'iron deficiency' argument. The 'range' of food that 'a vegetarian can eat' is stressed because 'there is nothing difficult about it and no self denial'.
2. (a) The language is sometimes highly emotive and carefully aimed at young people. For instance, 'Eat nothing but meat and you will die – and fairly quickly. Eat a variety of plant foods – fruits, vegetables, grains, nuts and seeds – and you will blossom.' There is the main slogan, 'You are what you eat'; young people are directly addressed in the second person, 'you', and there are some rhetorical questions to engage their youthful audience.
   (b) For instance, Viva! achieves this through friendly fonts, by varying the use of colour to represent a 'healthy' range of fruit and vegetables as well as their images, columns and bullet points make complex information very accessible. 'You are what you eat' straddles two sets of ideas: the arguments are mostly on left hand columns and the examples of the alternative foods are usually on the right.

Section B: Writing section
To get a top grade in writing question you will need to do the following:
- plan your writing
- focus on your audience and purpose and use appropriate language and tone
- develop points into logical, well-constructed paragraphs with topic sentences.
- use varied sentence structure and punctuation, as well as show clarity
- show a range of grammatical constructions
- employ a wide though appropriate vocabulary
- use a precise, fluent style
- show accuracy in your spelling and punctuation
- proof-read your work.

Index